Congregation for Institutes
of Consecrated Life and
Societies of Apostolic Life

FRATERNAL LIFE
IN
COMMUNITY

*Congregavit nos
in unum Christi amor*

Rome 1994

ST. PAUL BOOKS & MEDIA

BOSTON

Vatican Translation

ISBN 0-8198-2658-8

Printed and published by Pauline Books & Media, 50 St. Paul's Avenue, Boston, MA 02130.

Pauline Books & Media is the publishing house of the Daughters of St. Paul, an international congregation of women religious serving the Church with the communications media.

2 3 4 5 6   99 98 97 96 95

ABBREVIATIONS

Documents of the Second Vatican Council

DV   Dogmatic Constitution *Dei Verbum,* 1965.

GS   Pastoral Constitution *Gaudium et Spes,* 1965.

LG   Dogmatic Constitution *Lumen Gentium,* 1964.

PC   Decree *Perfectae Caritatis*, 1965.

PO   Decree *Presbyterorum Ordinis,* 1965.

SC   Constitution *Sacrosanctum Concilium,* 1963.

Pontifical Commission

ChL   Apostolic Exhortation *Christifideles Laici,* John Paul II, 1989.

EN   Apostolic Exhortation *Evangelii Nuntiandi,* Paul VI, 1975.

ET   Apostolic Exhortation *Evangelica Testificatio,* Paul VI, 1971.

MD   Apostolic Letter *Mulieris Dignitatem,* John Paul II, 1988.

MM   Encyclical Letter *Mater et Magistra,* John XXIII, 1961.

Documents of the Holy See

can.

canon

Canon   from the *Code of Canon Law,* 1983.

CDim *The Contemplative Dimension of Religious Life,* Sacred Congregation for Religious and Secular Institutes, SCRIS, 1980.

EE   *Essential Elements in the Church's Teaching on Religious Life*, SCRIS, 1983.

MR   *Directives for the Mutual Relations Between Bishops and Religious in the Church,* Sacred Congregation for Bishops and SCRIS, 1978.

PI   *Potissimum Institutioni, Directives on Formation in Religious Institutes* CICLSAL, 1990.

RHP   *Religious and Human Promotion*, SCRIS, 1980.

Other Abbreviations

CICLSAL Congregation for Institutes of Consecrated Life and
Societies of Apostolic Life.

OR   *L'Osservatore Romano.*

SD   *Santo Domingo: Conclusions of the IV General Assembly of the
Latin American Episcopate*, 1992.

In this text, "fraternal" and "fraternity" refer inclusively to both women and
men and are, in the judgment of the translators, the words most apt in
English for conveying the fullness and warmth of communion which lies at
the heart of community.

CONTENTS

PART I
THE GIFT OF COMMUNION
AND THE GIFT OF COMMUNITY

PART II
RELIGIOUS COMMUNITY AS THE PLACE
FOR BECOMING BROTHERS AND SISTERS

PART III
RELIGIOUS COMMUNITY AS THE PLACE
AND SUBJECT OF MISSION

INTRODUCTION

"Congregavit nos in unum Christi amor"

1. The love of Christ has gathered a great number of disciples to become one, so that like him and thanks to him, in the Spirit they might, throughout the centuries, be able to respond to the love of the Father, loving him "with all their hearts, with all their soul, with all their might" (cf. *Deut* 6:5) and loving their neighbors "as themselves" (cf. *Mt* 22:39).

Among these disciples, those gathered together in religious communities, women and men "from every nation, from all tribes and peoples and tongues" (*Rev* 7:9), have been and still are a particularly eloquent expression of this sublime and boundless love.

Born not "of the will of the flesh," nor from personal attraction, nor from human motives, but "from God" (*Jn* 1:13), from a divine vocation and a divine attraction, religious communities are a living sign of the primacy of the love of God who works wonders, and of the love for God and for one's brothers and sisters as manifested and practiced by Jesus Christ.

In view of the relevance of religious communities for the life and holiness of the Church, it is important to examine the lived experience of today's religious communities, whether monastic and contemplative or dedicated to apostolic activity, each according to its own specific character. All that is said here about religious communities applies also to communities in societies of apostolic life, bearing in mind their specific character and proper legislation.

a) The subject of this document is considered in light of this fact: the character which "fraternal life in common" manifests in numerous countries reveals many transformations of what was lived in the past. These transformations, as well as the hopes and disappointments which have accompanied them, and continue to do so, require reflection in light of the Second Vatican Council. The transformations have led to positive results, but also to results which are questionable. They have put into a clearer light not a few Gospel values, thus giving new vitality to religious community, but they have also given rise to questions by obscuring some elements characteristic of this same fraternal life lived in community. In some places, it seems that religious community has lost its relevance in the eyes of women and men religious and is, perhaps, no longer an ideal to be pursued.

With the serenity and urgency characteristic of those who seek the Lord, many communities have sought to evaluate this transformation, so that they might better fulfill their proper vocation in the midst of the People of God.

b) There are many factors that have determined the changes of which we are witnesses:

—"Constant return to the sources of the whole of the Christian life and to the primitive inspiration of the institutes."[1] This deeper and fuller encounter with the Gospel and with the first breakthrough of the foundational charism has been a vigorous impulse towards acquiring the true spirit which animates fraternity, and towards the structures and usages

---

1. *PC 2.*

which must express it adequately. Where the encounter with these sources and with the originating inspiration has been partial or weak, fraternal life has run risks and suffered a certain loss of tone.

—But this process has occurred within the context of other more general developments which are, as it were, its existential framework, and religious life cannot exempt itself from their repercussions.[2]

Religious life is a vital part of the Church and lives in the world. The values and counter-values which ferment within an epoch or a cultural setting, and the social structures which manifest them, impinge on everyone, including the Church and its religious communities. Religious communities either constitute an evangelical leaven within society, announce the Good News in the midst of the world—the here and now proclamation of the heavenly Jerusalem—or else they succumb by decline quickly or slowly, simply because they have conformed to the world. For this reason, a reflection and new proposals on "fraternal life in common" must take this existential framework into account.

—Developments within the Church have also marked religious communities deeply. The Second Vatican Council, as an event of grace and the greatest expression of the Church's pastoral guidance in this century, has had a decisive influence on religious life; not only by virtue of the Decree *Perfectae Caritatis,* which is dedicated to it, but also by virtue of the Council's ecclesiology, and each of its documents.

For all these reasons, this document, before addressing its

---

2. Cf. *PC* 2-4.

topic directly, begins with an overview of the changes encountered in the settings which have more immediately affected the quality of fraternal life and its ways of being lived in the various religious communities.

Theological Development

2. The Second Vatican Council contributed greatly to a re-evaluation of "fraternal life in common" and to a renewed vision of religious community.

More than any other factor, it is *the development of ecclesiology* which has affected the evolution of our understanding of religious community. Vatican II affirmed that religious life belongs "undeniably" (*inconcusse*) to the life and holiness of the Church and placed religious life at the very heart of the Church's mystery of communion and holiness.[3]

Religious community thus participates in the renewed and deepened vision of the Church. From this, several consequences follow:

a) From Church-mystery to the mystery dimension of religious community

Religious community is not simply a collection of Christians in search of personal perfection. Much more deeply, it is a participation in and qualified witness of the Church-mystery, since it is a living expression and privileged fulfillment of its own particular "communion," of the great Trinitarian *"koinonia,"* in which the Father has willed that men and women have part in the Son and in the Holy Spirit.

---

3. Cf. *LG* 44d.

*b) From Church-communion to the communional-fraternal
dimension of religious community*

Religious community, in its structure, motivations, and distinguishing values, makes publicly visible and continually perceptible the gift of fraternity given by Christ to the whole Church. For this very reason, it has as its commitment and mission, which cannot be renounced, both to be and to be seen as a living organism of intense fraternal communion, a sign and stimulus for all the baptized.[4]

*c) From Church animated by charisms to the charismatic
dimension of religious community*

Religious community is a living organism of fraternal communion, called to live as animated by the foundational charism. It is part of the organic communion of the whole Church, which is continuously enriched by the Spirit with a variety of ministries and charisms.

Those who enter into such communities must have the particular grace of a vocation. In practice, the members of a religious community are seen to be bound by *a common calling from God* in continuity with the *foundational charism,* by a characteristically common ecclesial consecration, and by a common response in sharing that "experience of the Spirit" lived and handed on by the founder and in his or her mission within the Church.[5]

The Church also wishes to receive with gratitude "the more

---

4 Cf. *PC* 15a; *LG* 44c.
5. Cf. *MR* 11.

simple and widely diffused" charisms[6] which God distributes among her members for the good of the entire Body. Religious community exists to be a sign of the Church and to enrich her,[7] to render her better able to carry out her mission.

d) From Church as sacrament of unity to the apostolic dimension of religious community

The purpose of apostolate is to bring humanity back to union with God and to unity among itself, through divine charity. Fraternal life in common, as an expression of the union effected by God's love, in addition to being an essential witness for evangelization, has great significance for apostolic activity and for its ultimate purpose. It is from this that the fraternal communion of religious community derives its vigor as sign and instrument. In fact, fraternal communion is at both the beginning and the end of apostolate.

The Magisterium, since the time of the Council, has deepened and enriched the renewed vision of religious community with fresh insights.[8]

Canonical Development

3. The Code of Canon Law (1983) specifies and defines the Council's determinations concerning community life.

When it speaks of "common life," it is necessary to distinguish clearly two aspects.

While the 1917 Code[9] could have given the impression of

---

6. *LG* 12.

7. Cf. *MR* 14.

8. Cf. *ET* 30-39; *MR* 2, 3, 10, 14; *EE* 18-22; *PI* 25-28; see also can. 602.

9. Cf. can. 594 § 1.

concentrating on exterior elements and uniformity of lifestyle, Vatican II[10] and the new Code[11] insist explicitly on the spiritual dimension and on the bond of fraternity which must unite all members in charity. The new Code has synthesized these two elements in speaking of "living a fraternal life in common."[12]

Thus, in community life, two elements of union and of unity among the members can be distinguished:

—one, the more spiritual: "fraternity" or "fraternal communion," which arises from hearts animated by charity. It underlines "communion of life" and interpersonal relationships;[13]

—the other, more visible: "life in common" or "community life," which consists of "living in one's own lawfully constituted religious house" and in "leading a common life" through fidelity to the same norms, taking part in common acts, and collaboration in common services.[14]

All of this is lived "in their own special manner"[15] in the various communities, according to the charism and proper law of the institute.[16] From this arises the importance of proper law which must apply to community life the patrimony of every institute and the means for doing this.[17]

It is clear that "fraternal life" will not automatically be achieved by observance of the norms which regulate common life; but it is evident that common life is designed to favor fraternal life greatly.

---

10. Cf. *PC* 15.
11. Cf. can. 602, 619.
12. Can. 607 § 2.
13. Cf. can. 602.
14. Cf. can. 608; 665 § 1.
15. Can. 731 § 1.
16. Cf. can. 607 § 2; also can. 602.
17. Cf. can. 587.

Development Within Society

4. Society is in constant evolution, and men and women religious—who are not of the world, but who nevertheless live in the world—are subject to its influence.

Here we will mention only some aspects which have had a direct impact on religious life in general and on religious community in particular.

a) Movements for political and social emancipation in the Third World and a stepped-up process of industrialization have led to the rise of major social changes, with particular emphasis on the "development of peoples" and, in recent decades, on situations of poverty and misery. Local Churches have reacted actively in the face of these developments.

Above all in Latin America, through the general assemblies of the Latin American episcopate at *Medellin, Puebla,* and *Santo Domingo,* the "evangelical and preferential option for the poor"[18] has been strongly emphasized, and has led to a new emphasis on social commitment.

Religious communities have been profoundly affected by this; many were led to rethink their presence in society, in view of more direct service to the poor, sometimes even through insertion among the poor.

The overwhelming increase of suffering on the outskirts of large cities and the impoverishment of rural areas have hastened the "repositioning" of a considerable number of religious communities towards these poorer areas.

Everywhere, there is the challenge of inculturation. Cultures, traditions, and the mentality of a particular country all have an impact on the way fraternal life is lived in religious communities.

---

18. *SD* 178, 180.

Moreover, movements of large-scale migration in recent years have raised the problem of the co-existence of different cultures, and the problem of racist reactions. All of these issues also have repercussions on pluri-cultural and multi-racial religious communities, which are becoming increasingly common.

b) Demands for personal freedom and human rights have been at the root of a broad process of democratization, which has favored economic development and the growth of civil society.

In the immediate wake of the Council, this process, especially in the west, quickened and was marked by moments of calling meetings about everything and rejection of authority.

The Church and religious life were not immune from such questioning of authority, with significant repercussions for community life as well.

A one-sided and exasperated stress on freedom contributed to the spread of a culture of individualism throughout the west, thus weakening the ideal of life in common and commitment to community projects.

We also observe other reactions which were equally one-sided, such as flight into safely authoritarian projects, based on blind faith in a reassuring leader.

c) The advancement of women, which according to Pope John XXIII is one of the signs of our times, has also had many repercussions on life in Christian communities in various countries.[19] Even if in some areas the influence of extremist currents of feminism is deeply affecting religious life, almost everywhere women's religious communities are positively seeking forms of common life judged more suitable for a renewed awareness of the identity, dignity and role of women

---

19. Cf. *Mulieris Dignitatem; GS* 9, 60.

in society, Church, and religious life.

d) The communications explosion, which began in the 1960's, has considerably—and at times dramatically—influenced the general level of information, the sense of social and apostolic responsibility, apostolic mobility and the quality of internal relationships, not to mention the specific lifestyle and recollected atmosphere which ought to characterize a religious community.

e) Consumerism and hedonism, together with a weakening of the vision of faith characteristic of secularism, in many regions have not left religious communities unaffected. These factors have severely tested the ability of some religious communities to "resist evil" but they have also given rise to new styles of personal and community life which are a clear evangelical testimony for our world.

All of this has been a challenge, a call to live the evangelical counsels with more vigor, and this has helped support the witness of the wider Christian community.

Changes in Religious Life

5. In recent years, there have been changes which have profoundly affected religious communities.

a) A new profile in religious communities. In many countries, increased state programs in areas in which religious have traditionally been active—such as social service, education, and health—together with the decrease in vocations, have resulted in a diminished presence of religious in works which used to be typically those of apostolic institutes.

Thus, there is a shrinking of large religious communities at the service of visible works which characterized various institutes for many years.

This is accompanied, in some regions, by a preference for smaller communities composed of religious who are active in works not belonging to the institute, even though they are often in line with the charism of that institute. This has a significant impact on the style of their common life and requires a change in traditional rhythms.

Sometimes the sincere desire to serve the Church and attachment to the institute's works, combined with urgent requests from the particular Church, can easily bring religious to take on too much work, thus leaving less time for common life.

b) The increase in the number of requests for assistance in responding to more urgent needs (those of the poor, drug addicts, refugees, the marginalized, the handicapped, the sick of every kind) has given rise in religious life to responses of admirable and admired dedication.

This, however, has also made evident the need for changes in the traditional profile of religious communities, which are deemed, by some, to be inadequate for coping with the new situations.

c) The way of understanding and living one's own work in a secularized context, especially when it is understood as the mere exercise of a given profession or occupation rather than as the undertaking of a mission of evangelization, has at times obscured the reality of consecration and the spiritual dimension of religious life, to the point that fraternal life in common has become for some an obstacle to the apostolate, or a merely functional instrument.

d) A *new concept of the human person* emerged in the immediate wake of the Council, emphasizing the value of the individual person and of personal initiatives. This was followed immediately by a sharpened sense of community, understood as fraternal life built more on the quality of interpersonal relationships than on the formal aspects of regular observance.

Here or there, these accents were radicalized (giving rise to the opposing tendencies of individualism and communitarianism), sometimes without coming to a satisfactory balance.

e) New governing structures emerged from revised constitutions, requiring far greater participation on the part of men and women religious. This has led to a different way of approaching problems, through community dialogue, co-responsibility and subsidiarity. All members became involved in the problems of the community. This greatly affected interpersonal relationships and, in turn, affected the way authority is perceived. In not a few cases, authority then encountered practical difficulties in finding its true place within the new context.

The combination of changes and tendencies mentioned has affected the character of religious communities in a profound way but also in ways that must be differentiated.

The differentiations, sometimes rather notable, depend, as can be easily understood, on the diversity of cultures and continents, on whether the communities are of men or of women, on the kind of religious life and the kind of institute, on the different activities and the degree of commitment to re-read and reclaim the charism of the founder, on the different ways of standing before society and the Church, on different ways of receiving the values proposed by the Council, on different traditions and ways of common life, and on various ways of exercising authority and promoting the renewal of permanent formation. These problematic settings are only partially common to all; rather they tend to differ from community to community.

Objectives of the Document

6. In light of these new situations, the purpose of this document is, above all, to support the efforts made by many communities of religious, both men and women, to improve the quality of their fraternal life. This will be done by offering some criteria of discernment, in view of authentic evangelical renewal.

This document also intends to offer reasons for reflection to those who have distanced themselves from the community ideal, so that they may give serious consideration again to the need for fraternal life in common for those consecrated to the Lord in a religious institute or incorporated in a society of apostolic life.

7. For this purpose, the document is structured as follows:

a) Religious community *as gift:* before being a human project, fraternal life in common is part of God's plan and he wishes to share his life of communion.

b) Religious community *as the place where we become brothers and sisters:* the most suitable channels for budding Christian fraternity by the religious community.

c) Religious community *as the place and subject of mission:* specific choices which a religious community is called to carry out in various situations, and criteria for discernment.

To enter into the mystery of communion and of fraternity, and before undertaking the difficult discernment necessary for renewing the evangelical radiance of our communities, we must humbly invoke the Holy Spirit, that he may accomplish what he alone can do: "I shall give you a new heart, and put a new spirit in you; I shall remove the heart of stone from your bodies and give you a heart of flesh instead. You shall be my people and I will be your God" (*Ez* 36:26-28).

PART I

THE GIFT OF COMMUNION
AND THE GIFT OF COMMUNITY

8. Before being a human construction, religious community is a gift of the Spirit. It is the love of God, poured into our hearts by the Holy Spirit, from which religious community takes its origin and is built as a true family gathered together in the Lord's name.[20]

It is therefore impossible to understand religious community unless we start from its being a gift from on high, from its being a mystery, from its being rooted in the very heart of the blessed and sanctifying Trinity, who wills it as part of the mystery of the Church, for the life of the world.

The Church as Communion

9. In creating man and woman in his own image and likeness, God created them for communion. God the Creator, who revealed himself as Love, as Trinity, as communion, called them to enter into intimate relationship with himself and into interpersonal communion, in the universal fraternity of all men and women.[21]

This is our highest vocation: to enter into communion with God and with our brothers and sisters.

God's plan was compromised through sin, which sundered every kind of relationship: between the human race and God,

---

20. Cf. *PC* 15a; can. 602.
21. Cf. *GS* 3.

between man and woman, among brothers and sisters, between peoples, between humanity and the rest of creation.

In his great love, the Father sent his Son, the new Adam, to reconstitute all creation and bring it to full unity. When he came among us, he established the beginning of the new People of God, calling to himself apostles and disciples, men and women—a living parable of the human family gathered together in unity. He announced to them universal fraternity in the Father, who made us his intimates, his children, and brothers and sisters among ourselves. In this way he taught equality in fraternity and reconciliation in forgiveness. He overturned the relationships of power and domination, himself giving the example of how to serve and choose the last place. During the Last Supper, he entrusted to them the new commandment of mutual love: "a new commandment I give to you, that you love one another; even as I have loved you, that you also love one another" (*Jn* 13:34; cf. 15:12); he instituted the Eucharist, which, making us share in the one bread and one cup, nourishes mutual love. Then he turned to the Father asking, as a synthesis of his desires, for the unity of all, modeled on the Trinitarian unity: "that they may all be one; even as you, Father, are in me and I in you, that they also may be in us" (cf. *Jn* 17:21).

Entrusting himself then to the Father's will, he achieved in the paschal mystery that unity which he had taught his disciples to live and which he had asked of the Father. By his death on the cross, he destroyed the barrier that separated peoples, reconciling us all in unity (cf. *Eph* 2:14-16). By this, he taught us that communion and unity are the fruit of sharing in the mystery of his death.

The coming of the Holy Spirit, first gift to believers, brought about the unity willed by Christ. Poured out on the disciples gathered in the Upper Room with Mary, the Spirit gave visibility to the Church, which, from the very first moment, is characterized as fraternity and communion in the unity of one heart and one soul (cf. *Acts* 4:32).

This communion is the bond of charity which joins among themselves all the members of the same Body of Christ, and the Body with its Head. The same life-giving presence of the Holy Spirit[22] builds in Christ organic cohesion: he unifies the Church in communion and ministry, coordinates and directs it with various hierarchic and charismatic gifts which complement each other, and makes the Church beautiful by his fruits.[23]

In her pilgrimage through this world, the Church, one and holy, has constantly been characterized by a tension, often painful, towards effective unity. Along her path through history, she has become increasingly conscious of being the People and family of God, the Body of Christ, Temple of the Spirit, Sacrament of the intimate union of the human race, communion, icon of the Trinity. The Second Vatican Council has brought out, perhaps as never before, this mysterious and "communional" dimension of the Church.

Religious Community as Expression of Ecclesial Communion

10. From the very beginning, consecrated life has cultivated this intimate nature of Christianity. In fact, the religious community has felt itself to be in continuity with the group of those who followed Jesus. He had called them personally, one by one, to live in communion with himself and with the other

---

22. Cf. *LG* 7.
23. Cf. *LG* 4; *MR* 2.

disciples, to share his life and his destiny (cf. *Mk* 3:13-15), and in this way to be a sign of the life and communion begun by him. The first monastic communities looked to the community of the disciples who followed Christ and to the community of Jerusalem as their ideal of life. Like the nascent Church, having one heart and one soul, so the monks, gathering themselves under a spiritual guide, the abbot, set out to live the radical communion of material and spiritual goods and the unity established by Christ. This unity finds its archetype and its unifying dynamism in the life of unity of the Persons of the Most Blessed Trinity.

In subsequent centuries, many forms of community have arisen under the charismatic action of the Spirit. He who searches the depths of the human heart reaches out to it and satisfies its needs. He raises up men and women who, enlightened by the light of the Gospel and sensitive to the signs of the times, give life to new religious families—and hence to new ways of living out the one single communion in a diversity of ministries and communities.[24]

It is impossible to speak of religious community univocally. The history of consecrated life witnesses to a variety of ways of living out the one communion according to the nature of the various institutes. Thus, today we can admire the "wondrous variety" of religious families which enrich the Church and equip her for every good work[25] and, deriving from this, the variety of forms of religious communities.

Nevertheless, in the various forms it takes, fraternal life in common has always appeared as a radical expression of the common fraternal spirit which unites all Christians. Religious

---

24. Cf. *PC* 1; *EF* 18-22.
25. Cf. *PC* 1.

community is a visible manifestation of the communion which is the foundation of the Church and, at the same time, a prophecy of that unity towards which she tends as her final goal. As "experts in communion, religious are, therefore, called to be an ecclesial community in the Church and in the world, witnesses and architects of the plan for unity which is the crowning point of human history in God's design. Above all, by profession of the evangelical counsels, which frees one from what might be an obstacle to the fervor of charity, religious are communally a prophetic sign of intimate union with God, who is loved above all things. Furthermore, through the daily experience of communion of life, prayer and apostolate—the essential and distinctive elements of their form of consecrated life—they are a sign of fraternal fellowship. In fact, in a world frequently very deeply divided and before their brethren in the faith, they give witness to the possibility of a community of goods, of fraternal love, of a program of life and activity which is theirs because they have accepted the call to follow more closely and more freely Christ the Lord who was sent by the Father so that, firstborn among many brothers and sisters, he might establish a new fraternal fellowship in the gift of his Spirit."[26]

This will be all the more visible to the extent that they not only think with and within the Church, but also feel themselves to be Church, identifying themselves with her in full communion with her doctrine, her life, her pastors, her faithful, her mission in the world.[27]

Particularly significant is the witness offered by contemplative men and women. For them, fraternal life has broader and deeper dimensions which derive from the

---

26. *RHP* 24.
27. *PI* 21-22.

fundamental demand of this special vocation, the search for God alone in silence and prayer.

Their constant attention to God makes their attention to other members of the community more delicate and respectful, and contemplation becomes a force liberating them from every form of selfishness.

Fraternal life in common, in a monastery, is called to be a living sign of the mystery of the Church: the greater the mystery of grace, so much the richer is the fruit of salvation.

In this way, the Spirit of the Lord, who gathered together the first believers, and who continually calls the Church into one single family, calls together and nourishes religious families which, by means of their communities spread throughout the world, have the mission of being clearly readable signs of that intimate communion which animates and constitutes the Church, and of being a support for the fulfillment of God's plan.

PART II

RELIGIOUS COMMUNITY AS THE PLACE FOR BECOMING BROTHERS AND SISTERS

11. From the gift of communion arises the duty to build fraternity, in other words, to become brothers and sisters in a given community where all are called to live together. From accepting with wonder and gratitude the reality of divine communion shared with mere creatures, there also arises conviction of the need to make it always more visible by building communities "filled with joy and with the Holy Spirit" (*Acts* 13:52).

In our days, and for our days, it is necessary to take up again this "divine-human" work of building up the community of brothers and sisters, keeping in mind the specific circumstances of present times in which theological, canonical, social and structural developments have profoundly affected the profile and life of religious community.

Starting from a number of specific situations, the present document wishes to offer indications for strengthening commitment to a continued evangelical renewal of communities.

Spirituality and Community Prayer

12. In its primary mystical component, every authentic Christian community is seen in "itself a theological reality, an object of contemplation."[28] It follows that a religious community is, above all else, a mystery which must be contem-

---

28. *CDim* 15.

plated and welcomed with a heart full of gratitude in the clear context of faith.

Whenever we lose sight of this mystical and theological dimension which binds religious community to the mystery of divine communion, present and communicated to the community, we inevitably come to forget the profound reasons for "making community," for patiently building fraternal life. This life can sometimes seem beyond human strength and a useless waste of energy, especially to those intensely committed to action and conditioned by an activistic and individualistic culture.

The same Christ who called them, daily calls together his brothers and sisters to speak with them and to unite them to himself and to each other in the Eucharist, to assimilate them increasingly into his living and visible Body, in whom the Spirit lives, on journey towards the Father.

Prayer in common, which has always been considered the foundation of all community life, starts from contemplation of God's great and sublime mystery, from wonder for his presence, which is at work in the most significant moments of the life of our religious families as well as in the humble and ordinary realities of our communities.

13. As a response to the admonition of the Lord, "watch at all times, and pray" (cf. *Lk* 21:36), a religious community needs to be watchful and take the time necessary for attending to the quality of its life. Sometimes men and women religious "don't have time" and their day runs the risk of being too busy and anxious, and the religious can end up being tired and exhausted. In fact, religious community is regulated by a rhythmic horarium to give determined times to prayer, and especially so that one can learn to give time to God (*vacare Deo*).

Prayer needs to be seen also as time for being with the Lord so that he might act in us and, notwithstanding distractions and weariness, might enter our lives, console them and guide them. So that, in the end, our entire existence can belong to him.

14. One of the most valuable achievements of recent decades, recognized and blessed by all, has been the rediscovery of liturgical prayer by religious families.

Communal celebration of the Liturgy of the Hours, or at least of some part of it, has revitalized prayer in many communities, which have been brought into more lively contact with the word of God and the prayer of the Church.[29]

Thus, all must remain strongly convinced that community is built up starting from the liturgy, especially from celebration of the Eucharist[30] and the other sacraments. Among these other sacraments, renewed attention should be given to the Sacrament of Reconciliation, through which the Lord restores union with himself and with one's brothers and sisters.

As happened in the first community in Jerusalem (cf. *Acts* 2:42), the word, the Eucharist, common prayer, dedication and fidelity to the teaching of the Apostles and their successors, put one in touch with God's great works; in this context, these works become resplendent and give rise to praise, thanksgiving, joy, union of hearts, comfort in the shared difficulties of daily life together, and mutual encouragement in faith.

Unfortunately, the decrease in the number of priests may, here or there, make it impossible to participate daily in the Mass. In these circumstances, we must be concerned to deepen our appreciation of the great gift of the Eucharist and place at the very heart of our lives the Sacred Mystery of the Body and Blood of our Lord, alive and present in the community to sustain and inspire it in its journey to the Father. From this derives the

---

29. Cf. can. 663 § 3 and 608.
30. Cf. *PO* 6; *PC* 6.

necessity that every religious house have its own oratory as the center of the community,[31] where members can nourish their own Eucharistic spirituality by prayer and adoration.

It is around the Eucharist, celebrated or adored, "source and summit" of all activity of the Church, that the communion of souls is built up, which is the starting point of all growth in fraternity. "From this all education for community spirit must begin."[32]

15. Communal prayer reaches its full effectiveness when it is intimately linked to personal prayer. Common prayer and personal prayer are closely related and are complementary to each other. Everywhere, but especially so in some regions and cultures, greater emphasis must be placed on the inner aspect, on the filial relationship to the Father, on the intimate and spousal relationship with Christ, on the personal deepening of what is celebrated and lived in community prayer, on the interior and exterior silence that leaves space for the Word and the Spirit to regenerate the more hidden depths. The consecrated person who lives in community nourishes his or her consecration both through constant personal dialogue with God and through community praise and intercession.

16. In recent years, community prayer has been enriched by various forms of expression and sharing.

For many communities, the sharing of *Lectio divina* and reflection on the word of God, as well as the sharing of personal faith experiences and apostolic concerns have been particularly fruitful. Differences of age, formation, and character make it advisable to be prudent in requiring this of an entire community. It is well to recall that the right moment cannot be rushed.

---

31. Cf. can. 608.
32. *PO* 6.

Where it is practiced with spontaneity and by common agreement, such sharing nourishes faith and hope as well as mutual respect and trust; it facilitates reconciliation and nourishes fraternal solidarity in prayer.

17. The Lord's injunction to "always pray and not lose heart" (*Lk* 18: 1; cf. *1 Thes* 5:17) is equally valid for personal prayer and for communal prayer. A religious community lives constantly in the sight of its Lord and ought to be continuously aware of his presence. Nevertheless, prayer in common has its own rhythms whose frequency (daily, weekly, monthly or yearly) is set forth in the proper law of each institute.

Prayer in common which requires fidelity to an horarium, also and above all requires perseverance: "that by steadfastness and by the encouragement of the scriptures we might have hope..., that together you may with one voice glorify the God and Father of our Lord Jesus Christ" (*Rom* 15:4-6).

Faithfulness and perseverance will also help overcome— creatively and wisely—certain difficulties which mark some communities, such as diversity of commitments and consequent differences in schedules, overwork which absorbs one, and various kinds of fatigue.

18. Prayer to the Blessed Virgin Mary, animated by a love for her which leads us to imitate her, has the effect that her exemplary and maternal presence becomes a great support in daily fidelity to prayer (cf. *Acts* 1:14), becoming a bond of communion for the religious community.[33]

The Mother of the Lord will help configure religious communities to the model of "her" family, the Family of Nazareth, a place which religious communities ought often to visit spiritually, because there the Gospel of communion and fraternity was lived in a wonderful way.

---

33. Cf. can. 663 § 4.

19. Common prayer also sustains and nourishes apostolic impulse. On the one hand, prayer is a mysterious transforming power which embraces all realities to redeem and order the world. On the other, it finds its stimulus in the apostolic ministry, in its daily joys and difficulties. These then become an occasion for seeking and discovering the presence and action of the Lord.

20. Religious communities which are most apostolically and evangelically alive—whether contemplative or active—are the ones which have a rich experience of prayer. At a time such as ours, when we note a certain reawakening of the search for the transcendent, religious communities can become privileged places where the various paths which lead to God can be experienced.

"As a family united in the Lord's name, [a religious community] is of its nature the place where the experience of God should be able in a special way to come to fullness and be communicated to others,"[34] above all to one's own brothers and sisters within the community.

Men and women consecrated to God will fail to meet this historic challenge if they do not respond to the "search for God" in our contemporaries, who will then perhaps turn to other erroneous paths in an effort to satisfy their thirst for the Absolute.

Personal Freedom and the Building of Fraternity

21. "Bear one another's burdens, and so fulfill the law of Christ" (*Gal* 6:2). In the entire dynamic of community life, Christ, in his paschal mystery, remains the model of how to construct unity. Indeed, he is the source, the model, and the measure of the command of mutual love: we must love one

---

34. *CDim* 15.

another as he loved us. And he loved us to the point of giving up his life for us. Our life is a sharing in the charity of Christ, in his love for the Father and for his brothers and sisters, a love forgetful of self.

All of this, however, is not in the nature of the "old man," who wants communion and unity but does not want or intend to pay the price in terms of personal commitment and dedication. The path that leads from the "old man," who tends to close in on himself, to the "new man" who gives himself to others is a long and difficult one. The holy founders realistically emphasized the difficulties and dangers of this passage, conscious as they were that community cannot be improvised. It is not a spontaneous thing nor is it achieved in a short time.

In order to live as brothers and sisters, a true journey of interior liberation is necessary. Israel, liberated from Egypt, became the People of God after walking for a long time through the desert under the guidance of Moses. In much the same way, a community inserted within the Church as People of God must be built by persons whom Christ has liberated and made capable of loving as he did, by the gift of his liberating love and the heartfelt acceptance of those he gives us as guides.

The love of Christ poured out in our hearts urges us to love our brothers and sisters even to the point of taking on their weaknesses, their problems, and their difficulties. In a word: even to the point of giving our very selves.

22. Christ gives a person two basic certainties: the certainty of being infinitely loved and the certainty of being capable of loving without limits. Nothing except the Cross of Christ can give in a full and definitive way these two certainties and the freedom they bring. Through them, consecrated persons gradually become free from the need to be at the center of

everything and to possess the other, and from the fear of giving themselves to their brothers and sisters. They learn rather to love as Christ loved them, with that love which now is poured forth in their hearts, making them capable of forgetting themselves and giving themselves as the Lord did.

By the power of this love a community is brought to life as a gathering of people who are free, liberated by the Cross of Christ.

23. This path of liberation which leads to full communion and to the freedom of the children of God demands, however, the courage of self-denial in accepting and welcoming the other with his or her limitations, starting with the acceptance of authority.

Many have noted that this has constituted one of the weak points of the recent period of renewal. There has been an increase of knowledge, and various aspects of communal life have been studied. Much less attention has been paid, however, to the ascetic commitment which is necessary and irreplaceable for any liberation capable of transforming a group of people into a Christian fraternity.

Communion is a gift offered which also requires a response, a patient learning experience and struggle, in order to overcome the excesses of spontaneity and the fickleness of desires. The highest ideal of community necessarily brings with it conversion from every attitude contrary to communion.

Community that is not mystical has no soul, but community that is not ascetic has no body. "Synergy" between the gift of God and personal commitment is required for building an incarnated communion, for giving, in other words, flesh and concrete existence to grace and to the gift of fraternal communion.

24. It must be admitted that this kind of reasoning presents difficulty today both to young people and to adults. Often, young people come from a culture which overrates subjectivity and the

search for self-fulfillment, while adults either are anchored to structures of the past or experience a certain disenchantment with respect to the never-ending assemblies which were prevalent some years ago, a source of verbosity and uncertainty.

If it is true that communion does not exist without the self-offering of each member, then it is necessary, right from the beginning, to remove the illusion that everything must come from others, and to help each one discover with gratitude all that has already been received, and is in fact being received from others. Right from the beginning, it is necessary to prepare to be not only consumers of community, but above all its builders; to be responsible for each other's growth; to be open and available to receive the gift of the other; to be able to help and to be helped; to replace and to be replaced.

A fraternal and shared common life has a natural attraction for young people but, later, perseverance in the real conditions of life can become a heavy burden. Initial formation needs, then, to bring one to awareness of the sacrifices required for living in community, to accepting them in view of a joyful and truly fraternal relationship and of all the other attitudes characteristic of one who is interiorly free.[35] When we lose ourselves for our brothers and sisters, then we find ourselves.

25. It must always be remembered that, for religious men and women, fulfillment comes through their communities. One who tries to live an independent life, detached from community, has surely not taken the secure path to the perfection of his or her own state.

Whereas western society applauds the independent person, the one who can attain self-actualization alone—the self-assured individualist, the Gospel requires persons who, like the grain of

---

35. Cf. *PI* 32-34; 87.

wheat, know how to die to themselves so that fraternal life may be born.[36]

Thus community becomes *"Schola Amoris,"* a School of Love, for young people and for adults—a school in which all learn to love God, to love the brothers and sisters with whom they live, and to love humanity, which is in great need of God's mercy and of fraternal solidarity.

26. The communitarian ideal must not blind us to the fact that every Christian reality is built on human frailty. The perfect "ideal community" does not exist yet: the perfect communion of the saints is our goal in the heavenly Jerusalem.

Ours is the time for edification and constant building. It is always possible to improve and to walk together towards a community that is able to live in forgiveness and love. Communities cannot avoid all conflicts. The unity which they must build is a unity established at the price of reconciliation.[37] Imperfection in communities ought not discourage us.

Every day, communities take up again their journey, sustained by the teaching of the Apostles: "love one another with brotherly affection; outdo one another in showing honor" (*Rom* 12:10); "live in harmony with one another" (*Rom* 12:16); "welcome one another, therefore, as Christ has welcomed you" (*Rom* 15:7); "I myself am satisfied...that you are...able to instruct one another" (*Rom* 15:14); "wait for one another" (*1 Cor* 11:33); "through love, be servants of one another" (*Gal* 5:13); "encourage one another" (*1 Thes* 5:11); "forbearing one another in love" (*Eph* 4:2); "be kind to one another, tenderhearted, forgiving one another" (*Eph* 4:32); "be subject to one another out of reverence for Christ" (*Eph* 5:21); "pray for one

---

36. Cf. *LG* 46b.
37. Cf. can, 602; *PC* 15a.

another" (*James* 5:16); "clothe yourselves, all of you, with humility towards one another" (*1 Pet* 5:5); "we have fellowship with one another" (*1 Jn* 1:7); "let us not grow weary in welldoing..., especially to those who are of the household of faith" (*Gal* 6:9-10).

27. It may be useful to recall that in order to foster communion of minds and hearts among those called to live together in a community, it is necessary to cultivate those qualities which are required in all human relationships: respect, kindness, sincerity, self-control, tactfulness, a sense of humor, and a spirit of sharing.

Recent documents from the Magisterium are rich with suggestions and indications helpful for community living such as joyful simplicity,[38] clarity and mutual trust,[39] capacity for dialogue,[40] and sincere acceptance of a beneficial communitarian discipline.[41]

28. We must not forget, in the end, that peace and pleasure in being together are among the signs of the Kingdom of God. The joy of living even in the midst of difficulties along the human and spiritual path and in the midst of daily annoyances is already part of the Kingdom. This joy is a fruit of the Spirit and embraces the simplicity of existence and the monotonous texture of daily life. A joyless fraternity is one that is dying out; before long, members will be tempted to seek elsewhere what they can no longer find within their own home. A fraternity rich in joy is a genuine gift from above to brothers and sisters who know how to ask for it and to accept one another, committing themselves to

---

38. Cf. *ET* 39.
39. Cf. *PC* 14.
40. Cf. can. 619.
41. Cf. *ET* 39; *FE* 19.

fraternal life, trusting in the action of the Spirit. Thus the words of the Psalm are made true: "Behold how good and pleasant it is when brothers dwell in unity.... For there the Lord has commanded the blessing, life for evermore" (*Ps* 133:1-3), "because when they live together as brothers, they are united in the assembly of the Church; they are of one heart in charity and of one will."[42]

Such a testimony of joy is a powerful attraction to religious life, a source of new vocations and an encouragement to perseverance. It is very important to cultivate such joy within a religious community: overwork can destroy it, excessive zeal for certain causes can lead some to forget it, constant self-analysis of one's identity and one's own future can cloud it.

Being able to enjoy one another; allowing time for personal and communal relaxation; taking time off from work now and then; rejoicing in the joys of one's brothers and sisters, in solicitous concern for the needs of brothers and sisters; trusting commitment to works of the apostolate; compassion in dealing with situations; looking forward to the next day with the hope of meeting the Lord always and everywhere: these are things that nourish serenity, peace and joy. They become strength in apostolic action.

Joy is a splendid testimony to the evangelical quality of a religious community; it is the end point of a journey which is not lacking in difficulties, but which is possible because it is sustained by prayer: "rejoice in your hope, be patient in tribulation, be constant in prayer" (*Rom* 12:12).

---

42. St. Hilary, Tract. in *Ps.* 132, *PL* Suppl. 1, 244.

Communicating in Order to Grow Together

29. In the renewal of recent years, communication has been recognized as one of the human factors acquiring increased importance for the life of a religious community. The deeply felt need to enhance fraternal life in community is accompanied by a corresponding need for communication which is both fuller and more intense.

In order to become brothers and sisters, it is necessary to know one another. To do this, it is rather important to communicate more extensively and more deeply. Today, more attention is given to various aspects of communication, although the form and the degree may vary from one institute to another, and from one region to the next.

30. Communication within institutes has developed considerably. There is a growing number of regular meetings of members at different levels, central, regional, and provincial; superiors often send letters and suggestions, and their visits to communities are more frequent. The publication of newsletters and internal periodicals is more widespread.

This kind of broad communication asked for at various levels, corresponding to the character proper to the institute, normally creates closer relations, nourishes a family spirit and a sharing in the concerns of the entire institute, creates greater sensitivity to general problems, and brings religious closer together around their common mission.

31. Regular meetings at the community level, often on a weekly basis, have also proved very useful; they let members share problems concerning the community, the institute, the Church, and in relation to the Church's major documents. They provide opportunities to listen to others, share one's own thoughts, review and evaluate past experiences, and think and plan together.

Such meetings are particularly necessary for the growth and development of fraternal life, especially in larger communities. Time must be set aside for this purpose and kept free from all other engagements. In addition to concern for community life, these meetings are also important for fostering co-responsibility and for situating one's own work within the broader framework of religious life, Church life, and the life of the world to which we are sent in mission. This is an avenue which must be pursued in every community, adapting its rhythms and approaches to the size of the community and to the members' commitments. In contemplative communities, it should respect their own style of life.

32. But there is more. In many places, there is a felt need for more intense communication among religious living together in the same community. The lack of or weakness in communication usually leads to weakening of fraternity: if we know little or nothing about the lives of our brothers or sisters, they will be strangers to us, and the relationship will become anonymous, as well as create true and very real problems of isolation and solitude. Some communities complain about the poor quality of the fundamental sharing of spiritual goods. Communication takes place, they say, around problems and issues of marginal importance but rarely is there any sharing of what is vital and central to the journey of consecration.

This can have painful consequences, because then spiritual experience imperceptibly takes on individualistic overtones. A mentality of self-sufficiency becomes more important; a lack of sensitivity to others develops; and gradually, significant relationships are sought outside the community.

This problem should be dealt with explicitly. It requires, on the one hand, a tactful and caring approach which does not exert pressure; but it also requires courage and creativity, searching for ways and methods which will make it possible for all to learn to share, simply and fraternally, the gifts of the Spirit so that these may indeed belong to all and be of benefit to all (cf. *1 Cor* 12:7).

Communion originates precisely in sharing the Spirit's gifts, a sharing of faith and in faith, where the more we share those things which are central and vital, the more the fraternal bond grows in strength. This kind of communication can also be helpful as a way of learning a style of sharing which will enable members, in their own apostolates, to "confess their faith" in simple and easy terms which all may understand and appreciate.

There are many ways in which spiritual gifts can be shared and communicated. Besides the ones already mentioned (sharing the word and the experience of God, communal discernment, community projects),[43] we should recall fraternal correction, review of life, and other forms characteristic of the tradition. These are concrete ways of putting at the service of others and of pouring into the community the gifts which the Spirit gives so abundantly for its upbuilding and for its mission in the world.

All of this takes on greater importance now since communities often include religious of different ages and different races, members with different cultural and theological formation, religious who have had widely differing experiences during these agitated and pluralistic years.

Without dialogue and attentive listening, community members run the risk of living juxtaposed or parallel lives, a far cry from the ideal of fraternity.

33. Every kind of communication implies itineraries and particular psychological difficulties which can also be addressed positively with the help of the human sciences. Some

---

43. See above nn. 14, 16, 28, and 31.

communities have benefited, for example, from the help of experts in communication and professionals in the fields of psychology or sociology.

These are exceptional measures which need to be evaluated prudently, and they can be used with moderation by communities wishing to break down the walls of separation which at times are raised within a community. These human techniques are useful, but they are not sufficient. All must have at heart the welfare of their brothers and sisters, cultivating an evangelical ability to receive from others all that they might wish to give and to communicate, and all that they in fact communicate by their very existence.

Be "of the same mind, having the same love, being in full accord and of one mind.... In humility count others better than yourselves. Let each of you look not only to his own interests, but also to the interests of others." Your mutual relations should be founded on the fact that you are united to Christ Jesus (cf. *Phil* 2:2-5).

In a climate such as this, various techniques and approaches to communication compatible with religious life can enhance the growth of fraternity.

34. The considerable impact of mass media on modern life and mentality has its effect on religious communities as well, and frequently affects internal communication.

A community, aware of the influence of the media, should learn to use them for personal and community growth, with the evangelical clarity and inner freedom of those who have learned to know Christ (cf. *Gal* 4:17-23). The media propose, and often impose, a mentality and model of life in constant contrast with the Gospel. In this connection, in many areas one hears of the desire for deeper formation in receiving and using the media both critically and fruitfully. Why not make them an object of evaluation, of discernment and of planning in the regular community meetings?

In particular when television becomes the only form of recreation, relations among people are blocked or even impeded, fraternal communication is limited and indeed consecrated life itself can be damaged.

A proper balance is needed: the moderate and prudent use of the communications media,[44] accompanied by community discernment can help the community know better the complexity of the world of culture, receive the media with awareness and a critical eye and, finally, evaluate their impact in relation to the various ministries at the service of the Gospel.

In keeping with the choice of their specific state of life, characterized by a more marked separation from the world, contemplative communities should consider themselves more committed to preserving an atmosphere of recollection, being guided by the norms determined in their own constitutions about the use of the communications media.

Religious Community and Personal Growth

35. Because religious community is a *Schola Amoris* which helps one grow in love for God and for one's brothers and sisters, it is also a place for human growth. The path is a demanding one, since it requires the renunciation of goods that are certainly highly valued,[45] but it is not impossible. A multitude of men and women saints and the wonderful figures of religious men and women are there to prove that consecration to

---

44. Cf. *CDim* 14; *PI* 13; can. 666.
45. *LG* 46.

Christ "does not constitute an obstacle to the true development of the human person but by its nature is supremely beneficial to that development."[46]

The path towards human maturity, which is a prerequisite of a radiant evangelical life, is a process which knows no limits, since it involves continuous enrichment not only of spiritual values but also of values in the psychological, cultural and social order.[47]

In recent years, major changes in culture and custom have been oriented, in practice, more towards material realities than towards spiritual values. This makes it necessary to pay attention to some areas where, today, persons appear to be particularly vulnerable.

36. *Identity*

The process of maturing takes place through one's own identifying with the call of God. A weak sense of identity can lead to a misconceived idea of self-actualization, especially in times of difficulty, with an excessive need for positive results and approval from others, an exaggerated fear of inadequacy, and depression brought on by failure.

The identity of a consecrated person depends on spiritual maturity; this is brought about by the Spirit who prompts us to be conformed to Christ, according to the particular characteristic provided by "the founding gift which mediates the Gospel to the members of a given religious institute."[48] For this reason, the help of a spiritual guide, who knows well and respects the spirituality and mission of the institute, is most important. Such a one will "discern the action of God, accompany the religious in the ways

---

46. *Ibid.*
47. Cf. *EE* 45.
48. *Ibid.*

of God, nourish life with solid doctrine and the practice of prayer."[49] This accompaniment is particularly necessary in the initial stage of formation, but it is useful throughout life, in order to foster "growth towards the fullness of Christ."

Cultural maturity also helps one face the challenges of mission by acquiring the tools necessary for discerning future trends and working out appropriate responses in which the Gospel is continuously proposed as the alternative to worldly proposals, integrating its positive forces and purifying them of the leaven of evil.

In this dynamic, the consecrated person and the religious community are a proposal of the Gospel, a proposal which manifests the presence of Christ in the world.[50]

37. *Affectivity*

Fraternal life in common requires from all members good psychological balance within which each individual can achieve emotional maturity. As mentioned above, one essential element of such growth is emotional freedom, which enables consecrated persons to love their vocation and to love in accordance with this vocation. It is precisely this freedom and this maturity which allow us to live out our affectivity correctly, both inside and outside the community.

To love one's vocation, to hear the call as something that gives true meaning to life, and to cherish consecration as a true, beautiful and good reality which gives truth, beauty and goodness to one's own existence all of this makes a person strong and autonomous, secure in one's own identity, free of the need for various forms of support and compensation, especially

---

49. *EE* 47.
50. Cf. *LG* 44.

in the area of affectivity. All this reinforces the bond that links the consecrated person to those who share his or her calling. It is with them, first and foremost, that he or she feels called to live relationships of fraternity and friendship.

To love one's vocation is to love the Church, it is to love one's institute, and to experience the community as one's own family.

To love in accordance with one's vocation is to love in the manner of one who, in every human relationship, wishes to be a clear sign of the love of God, not invading and not possessing, but loving and desiring the good of the other with God's own benevolence.

Therefore, special formation is required in the area of affectivity to promote an integration of the human aspect with the more specifically spiritual aspect. In this respect, the guidelines contained in *Potissimum Institutioni*[51] concerning discernment of "a balanced affectivity, especially sexual balance" and "the ability to live in community" are particularly relevant.

However, difficulties in this area are frequently echoes of problems originating in other areas: affectivity and sexuality marked by a narcissistic and adolescent attitude, or by rigid repression, can sometimes be a result of negative experiences prior to entering the community, but they can also be a result of difficulties in community or apostolate. A rich and warm fraternal life, one that "carries the burden" of the wounded brother or sister in need of help, is thus particularly important.

While a certain maturity is necessary for life in community, a cordial fraternal life is equally necessary in order to allow each religious to attain maturity. Where members of a community

---

51. *PI* 43.

become aware of diminished affective autonomy in one of their brothers or sisters, the response on the part of the community ought to be one of rich and human love, similar to that of our Lord Jesus and of many holy religious—a love that shares in fears and joys, difficulties and hopes, with that warmth that is particular to a new heart that knows how to accept the whole person. Such love—caring and respectful, gratuitous rather than possessive—should make the love of Our Lord seem very near: that love which caused the Son of God to proclaim through the Cross that we cannot doubt that we are loved by Love.

38. *Difficulties*

A special occasion for human growth and Christian maturity lies in living with persons who suffer, who are not at ease in community, and who thus are an occasion of suffering for others and of disturbance in community life.

We must first of all ask about the source of such suffering. It may be caused by a character defect, commitments that seem too burdensome, serious gaps in formation, excessively rapid changes over recent years, excessively authoritarian forms of government, or by spiritual difficulties.

There may be some situations when the one in authority needs to remind members that life in common sometimes requires sacrifice and can become a form of *maxima poenitentia*, grave penance.

In some cases recourse to the social sciences is necessary, in particular where individuals are clearly incapable of living community life due to problems of insufficient maturity and psychological weakness, or due to factors which are more pathological.

Recourse to such intervention has proved useful not only at the therapeutic stage—in cases of more or less evident psychopathology—but also as a preventive measure, to assist in the proper selection of candidates, and to assist formation teams in some cases to address specific pedagogical and formative problems.[52]

In all cases, in choosing specialists, preference is to be given to those who are believers and are well experienced with religious life and its dynamics. So much the better if these specialists are themselves consecrated men or women.

Finally, the use of such methods will be truly effective only if it is applied exceptionally and not generalized; this is so partly because psychopedagogical measures do not solve all problems and thus "cannot substitute for an authentic spiritual direction."[53]

From *Me* to *Us*

39. Respect for the human person, recommended by the Council and by various succeeding documents,[54] has had a positive influence on the praxis of communities. Simultaneously, however, individualism has spread, with greater or lesser intensity depending on the regions of the world, and in various forms: the need to take center stage; an exaggerated insistence on personal well-being, whether physical, psychological or professional; a preference for individual work or for prestigious and "signed" work; the absolute priority of one's personal aspirations and one's own individual path, regardless of others and with no reference to the community.

---

52. *PI* 43, 51, 63.
53. *PI* 52.
54. *PC* 14c; can. 618; *EE* 49.

On the other hand, we must continue to seek a just balance, not always easy to achieve, between the common good and respect for the human person, between the demands and needs of individuals and those of the community, between personal charisms and the community's apostolate. And this should be far from both the disintegrating forces of individualism and the leveling aspects of communitarianism. Religious community is the place where the daily and patient passage from "me" to "us" takes place, from my commitment to a commitment entrusted to the community, from seeking "my things" to seeking "the things of Christ."

In this way, religious community becomes the place where we learn daily to take on that new mind which allows us to live in fraternal communion through the richness of diverse gifts and which, at the same time, fosters a convergence of these gifts towards fraternity and towards co-responsibility in the apostolic plan.

40. In order to realize such a community and apostolic "symphony," it is necessary:

a) to celebrate and give thanks together for the common gift of vocation and mission, a gift far surpassing every individual and cultural difference; to promote a contemplative attitude with regard to the wisdom of God, who has sent specific brothers and sisters to the community that each may be a gift to the other; to praise him for what each brother or sister communicates from the presence and word of Christ;

b) to cultivate mutual respect by which we accept the slow journey of weaker members without stifling the growth of richer personalities; a respect which fosters creativity but also calls for responsibility to others and to solidarity;

c) to focus on a common mission: each institute has its own mission, to which all must contribute according to their particular gifts. The road of consecrated men and women consists precisely in progressively consecrating to the Lord all that they have, and all that they are, for the mission of their religious family;

d) to recall that the apostolic mission is entrusted in the first place to the community and that this often entails conducting works proper to the institute. Dedication to this kind of community apostolate helps a consecrated person mature and grow in his or her particular way of holiness;

e) to consider that religious, on receiving in obedience personal missions, ought to consider themselves sent by the community. For its part, the community shall see to their regular updating and include them in the reviews of apostolic and community commitments.

During the time of formation, all good will not withstanding, it may prove impossible to integrate the personal gifts of a consecrated individual within fraternity and a common mission. It may be necessary in such cases to ask, "Do God's gifts in this person...make for unity and deepen communion? If they do, they can be welcomed. If they do not, then no matter how good the gifts may seem to be in themselves, or how desirable they may appear to some members, they are not for this particular institute.... It is not wise to tolerate widely divergent lines of development which do not have a strong foundation of unity in the institute itself."[55]

41. In recent years, there has been an increase in the number of small communities, especially for reasons of apostolate. These communities can also foster closer relations among religious, prayer which is more deeply shared, and a reciprocal and more fraternal taking up of responsibility.[56]

---

55. *EE* 22; cf. also *MR* 12.
56. Cf. *ET* 40.

But there are some motives which are questionable, such as sameness of tastes or of mentality. In this situation, it is easy for a community to close in on itself and come to the point of choosing its own members, and brothers or sisters sent by the superiors may or may not be accepted. This is contrary to the very nature of religious community and to its function as sign. Optional homogeneity, besides weakening apostolic mobility, weakens the Pneumatic strength of a community and robs the spiritual reality which rules the community of its power as witness.

The effort involved in mutual acceptance and commitment to overcoming difficulties, characteristics of heterogeneous communities, show forth the transcendence of the reason which brought the community into existence, that is, the power of God which "is made perfect in weakness" (2 Cor 12:9-10).

We stay together in community not because we have chosen one another but because we have been chosen by the Lord.

42. Whereas culture of a western stamp can lead to individualism which makes fraternal life in common difficult, other cultures can lead to communitarianism which makes giving proper recognition to the human person difficult. All cultural forms need evangelization.

The presence of religious communities—which, through a process of conversion, enter into a fraternal life where individuals make themselves available to their brothers or sisters, and where the "group" enhances the individual—is a sign of the transforming power of the Gospel and of the coming of the Kingdom of God.

International institutes in which members from different cultures live together can contribute to an exchange of gifts through which the members mutually enrich and correct one other in the common desire to live more and more intensely the Gospel of personal freedom and fraternal communion.

Being a Community in Permanent Formation

43. Community renewal has greatly benefited from permanent formation. Recommended and presented in its basic outline by the document *Potissimum Institutioni*,[57] permanent formation is considered by all who are responsible for religious institutes as of vital importance for the future.

In spite of some uncertainties (difficulties in integrating its different aspects, difficulties in sensitizing all the members of a community, the absorbing demands of apostolic work, and a correct balance between activity and formation), most institutes, at either the central or local level, have undertaken initiatives.

One of the goals of such initiatives is to form communities that are mature, evangelical, fraternal, and capable of continuing permanent formation in daily life. Religious community is the place where broad guidelines are implemented concretely, through patient and persevering daily efforts. Religious community is, for everyone, the place and the natural setting of the process of growth, where all become co-responsible for the growth of others. Religious community is also the place where, day by day, members help one another to respond as consecrated persons, bearing a common charism, to the needs of the least and to the challenges of the new society.

Quite frequently, responses to existing problems can differ and this entails obvious consequences for community life. From this arises the realization that one of the challenges intensely felt today is to integrate members who were given a different formation and have different apostolic visions into one single community life, in such a way that these differences become not so much occasions of conflict as moments of mutual enrichment.

---

57. Cf. *PI* 66-69.

In such a diversified and changeable context, the unifying role of those responsible for community becomes ever more important; it is appropriate to provide them with specific support in the area of permanent formation, in light of their task of motivating the fraternal and apostolic life of their communities.

Based on the experience of recent years, two aspects deserve particular attention: the community dimension of the evangelical counsels and the charism.

44. *The Community Dimension of the Evangelical Counsels*

Religious profession expresses the gift of self to God and to the Church—a gift, however, which is lived in the community of a religious family. Religious are not only "called" to an individual personal vocation. Their call is also a "*con-vocation*"—they are called with others, with whom they share their daily life.

There is here a convergence of "yesses" to God which unites a number of religious into one single community of life. Consecrated together—united in the same "yes," united in the Holy Spirit—religious discover every day that their following of Christ, "obedient, poor and chaste," is lived in fraternity, as was the case with the disciples who followed Jesus in his ministry. They are united with Christ, and therefore called to be united among themselves. They are united in the mission to oppose prophetically the idolatry of power, of possession, and of pleasure.[58]

Thus, *obedience* binds together the various wills and unites them in one single fraternal community, endowed with a specific mission to be accomplished within the Church.

---

58. Cf. *RHP* 25.

Obedience is a "yes" to God's design, by which he has entrusted a particular task to a group of people. It brings with it a bond to the mission, but also to the community which must carry out its service here and now and together. It also requires a clear-sighted vision of faith regarding the superiors who "fulfill their duty of service and leadership"[59] and who are to see that there is conformity between apostolic work and the mission. It is in communion with them that the divine will—the only will which can save—must be fulfilled.

Poverty, the sharing of goods, even spiritual goods, has been from the beginning the basis of fraternal communion. The poverty of individual members, which brings with it a simple and austere lifestyle, not only frees them from the concerns inherent in private ownership but it also enriches the community, enabling it to serve God and the poor more effectively.

Poverty includes an economic dimension: the possibility of disposing of money as if it were one's own, either for oneself or for members of one's family, a lifestyle too different from that of fellow community members and from the poverty level of the society within which one is living—these things injure and weaken fraternal life.

"Poverty of spirit," humility, simplicity, recognizing the gifts of others, appreciating evangelical realities such as "the hidden life with Christ in God," respect for the hidden sacrifice, giving value to the least ones, dedication to efforts that are neither recognized nor paid—these are all unitive aspects of fraternal life and spring from the poverty professed.

A community of "poor" people is better able to show solidarity with the poor and to point to the very heart of evangelization because it concretely presents the transforming power of the beatitudes.

---

59. *MR* 13.

In the community dimension, consecrated *chastity*, which also implies great purity of mind, heart and body, expresses a great freedom for loving God and all that is his, with an undivided love and thus with a total availability for loving and serving all others, making present the love of Christ. This love, neither selfish nor exclusive, neither possessive nor enslaved to passion, but universal and disinterested, free and freeing, so necessary for mission, is cultivated and grows through fraternal life. Thus, those who live consecrated celibacy "recall that wonderful marriage made by God, which will be fully manifested in the future age, and in which the Church has Christ for her only spouse."[60]

This communal dimension of the vows must be continuously fostered and deepened—a process which is characteristic of permanent formation.

45. *The Charism*

This is the second aspect of permanent formation to which we must give special attention in order to promote the growth of fraternal life.

"Religious consecration establishes a particular communion between religious and God and, in him, between the members of the same institute.... The foundation of unity, however, is the communion in Christ established by the one founding gift."[61] Reference to the institute's founder and to the charism lived by him or her and then communicated, kept and developed throughout the life of the institute,[62] thus appears as an essential element for the unity of the community.

To live in community is to live the will of God together, in

---

60. *PC* 12; cf. can. 607.
61. *EE* 18; cf. *MR* 11-12
62. Cf. *MR* 11.

accordance with the orientation of the charismatic gift received by the founder from God and transmitted to his or her disciples and followers.

The renewal of recent years, re-emphasizing the importance of the originating charism by rich theological reflection,[63] has promoted the unity of the community, which is seen as bearer of this same gift from the Spirit, a gift to be shared with the brothers or sisters, and by which it is possible to enrich the Church "for the life of the world." For this reason, formation programs which include regular courses of study and prayerful reflection on the founder, the charism, and the constitutions of the institute are particularly beneficial.

A deepened understanding of the charism leads to a clearer vision of one's own identity, around which it is easier to build unity and communion. Clarity concerning one's own charismatic identity allows creative adjustment to new situations and this leads to positive prospects for the future of the institute.

A lack of clarity in this area can easily cause insecurity concerning goals and vulnerability in relation to conditions surrounding religious life, cultural currents and various apostolic needs; it may even make adaptation and renewal impossible.

46. It is therefore necessary to promote an institute's charismatic identity, especially to avoid a kind of *genericism*, which is a true threat to the vitality of a religious community.

Several factors have been identified as having caused suffering for religious communities in recent years and, in some cases, continue to cause it:

—a "generic" approach—in other words, one that lacks the

---

63. Cf. *MR* 11-12; *EE* 11; 41.

specific mediation of one's own charism—in considering certain guidelines of the particular Church or certain suggestions deriving from different spiritualities;

—a certain kind of involvement in ecclesial movements which exposes individual religious to the ambiguous phenomenon of "dual membership";

—in the essential and often fruitful relationships with laity, especially with lay collaborators, a certain adjustment to a lay mentality; instead of offering their own religious witness as a fraternal gift which would encourage Christian authenticity, they simply imitate the laity, taking on their way of seeing and acting, thus weakening the contribution of their own consecration;

—an excessive accommodation to the demands of family, to the ideals of nation, race or tribe, or of some social group, which risks distorting the charism to suit particular positions or interests.

The genericism which reduces religious life to a colorless, lowest common denominator leads to wiping out the beauty and fruitfulness of the many and various charisms inspired by the Holy Spirit.

Authority in the Service of Fraternity

47. It is generally agreed that the evolution of recent years has contributed to the maturity of fraternal life in communities. In many communities, the climate of life in common has improved: there is more space for the active participation of all; there has been a move from a common life based too much on observance to a life that is more attentive to individual needs, that is better attended to on the human level. The effort to build communities that are less formalistic, less authoritarian, more fraternal and participatory, is generally considered to be one of the more visible fruits of these recent years.

48. These positive developments in some places have risked being compromised by a distrust of authority.

The desire for deeper communion among the members and an understandable reaction against structures felt as being too rigid and authoritarian have contributed to a lack of understanding of the full scope of the role of authority; indeed, some consider it to be altogether unnecessary to community life, and others have reduced it to the simple role of coordinating the initiatives of the members. As a result, a certain number of communities have been led to live with no one in charge, while other communities make all decisions collegially. All of this brings with it the danger, not merely hypothetical, of a complete breakdown of community life; it tends to give priority to individual paths, and simultaneously to blur the function of authority—a function which is both necessary for the growth of fraternal life in community and for the spiritual journey of the consecrated person.

However, the results of these experiments are gradually leading back to a rediscovery of the need for and the role of personal authority, in continuity with the entire tradition of religious life.

If a widespread democratic climate has encouraged the growth of co-responsibility and of participation by all in the decision-making process, even within the religious community, nevertheless, we must not forget that fraternity is not only a fruit of human effort but also and above all a gift of God. It is a gift that comes from obedience to the Word of God, and also, in religious life, to the authority who reminds us of that Word and relates it to specific situations, in accordance with the spirit of the institute.

"But we beseech you, brothers, to respect those who labor among you and are over you in the Lord and admonish you, and to esteem them very highly in love because of their work" (*1 Thes* 5:12-13). The Christian community is not an anonymous collective, but it is endowed, from the beginning, with leaders, for whom the Apostle asks consideration, respect and charity.

In religious communities, authority, to whom attention and respect are due also by reason of the obedience professed, is placed at the service of the fraternity, of its being built up, of the achievement of its spiritual and apostolic goals.

49. The recent renewal has helped to redesign authority with the intention of linking it once again more closely to its evangelical roots and thus to the service of the spiritual progress of each one and the building up of fraternal life in community.

Every community has a mission of its own to accomplish. Persons in authority thus serve a community which must accomplish a specific mission, received and defined by the institute and by its charism. Since there is a variety of missions, there must also be a variety of kinds of communities, and thus a variety of ways of exercising authority. It is for this reason that religious life has within it various ways of conceiving and exercising authority, defined by proper law.

Authority is, evangelically, always service.

50. The renewal of recent years has led to highlighting some aspects of authority.

a) Spiritual Authority

If consecrated persons have dedicated themselves to the total service of God, authority promotes and sustains their consecration. In a certain sense, authority can be seen as "servant of the servants of God." Authority has as its main task building in unity the brothers and sisters of "a fraternal community, in which God is sought and loved above all."[64] A

---

64. Can. 619.

superior must therefore be, above all, a spiritual person, convinced of the primacy of the spiritual, both with respect to personal life and for the development of fraternal life; in other words, he or she must know that the more the love of God increases in each individual heart, the more unity there will be between hearts.

Thus, the superior's main task will be the spiritual, community, and apostolic animation of his or her community.

b) Authority Conducive to Unity

An authority conducive to unity is one concerned to create a climate favorable to sharing and co-responsibility; to encourage all to contribute to the affairs of all; to encourage members to assume and to respect responsibility; to promote, by their respect for the human person, voluntary obedience;[65] to listen willingly to the members, promoting their harmonious collaboration for the good of the institute and the Church;[66] to engage in dialogue and offer timely opportunities for encounter; to give courage and hope in times of difficulty; to look ahead and point to new horizons for mission. Still more: an authority which seeks to maintain a balance among the various aspects of community life—between prayer and work, apostolate and formation, work and rest.

The authority of a superior works so that the religious house is not merely a place of residence, a collection of subjects each of whom lives an individual history, but a "fraternal community in Christ."[67]

---

65. Cf. can. 618.
66. *Ibid.*
67. Can. 619.

c) Authority Capable of Making Final Decisions and Assuming Their Implementation

Community discernment is a rather useful process, even if not easy or automatic, for involving human competence, spiritual wisdom, and personal detachment. Where it is practiced with faith and seriousness, it can provide superiors with optimal conditions for making necessary decisions in the best interests of fraternal life and of mission.

When a decision has been made in accordance with the procedures established by proper law, superiors need perseverance and strength to ensure that what has been decided not remain mere words on paper.

51. It is also necessary that the proper law of each institute be as precise as possible in determining the respective competence of the community, the various councils, departmental coordinators and the superior. A lack of clarity in this area is a source of confusion and conflict.

"Community projects," which can help increase participation in community life and in its mission in various contexts, should also take care to define clearly the role and competence of authority, in line with the constitutions.

52. Fraternal and united communities are increasingly called to be an important and eloquent element of the Gospel counter-culture, salt of the earth and light of the world.

Thus, for example, if in western society where individualism is rampant, a religious community is called to be a prophetic sign of the possibility of achieving in Christ fraternity and solidarity, in cultures where authoritarianism or communitarianism is rampant it is called to be a sign of respect for and promotion of the human person, and also an exercise of authority in agreement with the will of God.

While religious communities must take on the culture of their place, they are also called to purify and elevate it, through the salt and light of the Gospel, offering through their existing communities a concrete synthesis of what is not only an evangelization of culture but also an evangelizing inculturation and an inculturated evangelization.

53. Finally, we must never forget in this delicate, complex, and often painful issue that faith plays a decisive role which allows us to understand the saving mystery of obedience.[68] Just as from the disobedience of one man came the disintegration of the human family and from the obedience of the New Man began its reconstitution (cf. *Rom* 5:19), so an obedient attitude will always be an essential force for all family life.

Religious life has always lived from this conviction of faith and is called to live from it also today with courage, so as not to run in vain in search of fraternal relations, and so as to be an evangelically relevant reality in the Church and in society.

Fraternity as Sign

54. The relationship between fraternal life and apostolic activity, in particular within institutes dedicated to works of the apostolate, has not always been clear and has all too often led to tension, both for the individual and for the community. For some, "building community" is felt as an obstacle to mission, almost a waste of time in matters of secondary importance. All must be reminded that fraternal communion, as such, is already an apostolate; in other words, it contributes directly to the work of evangelization. The sign *par excellence* left us by Our Lord is that of lived fraternity: "By this all will know that you are my

---

68. Cf. *PC* 14; *EE* 49.

disciples, if you have love for one another" (cf. *Jn* 13:35).

Along with sending them to preach the Gospel to every creature (*Mt* 28:19-20), the Lord sent his disciples to live together "so that the world may believe" that Jesus is the one sent by the Father and that we owe him the full assent of faith (*Jn* 17:21). The sign of fraternity is then of the greatest importance because it is the sign that points to the divine origin of the Christian message and has the power to open hearts to faith. For this reason, "the effectiveness of religious life depends on the quality of the fraternal life in common."[69]

55. A religious community, if and to the extent that it promotes fraternal life among its members, makes present in a continuous and legible way this "sign" which is needed by the Church, above all in her task of new evangelization.

Also for this reason, the Church takes to heart the fraternal life of religious communities: the more intense their fraternal love, the greater the credibility of the message she proclaims, and the more visible the heart of the mystery of the Church, sacrament of the union of humankind with God, and of its members among themselves.[70] Fraternal life is not the "entirety" of the mission of a religious community, but it is an essential element. Fraternal life is just as important as apostolic life.

The needs of apostolic service cannot therefore be invoked to accept or to justify defective community life. Activities undertaken by religious must be activities of people who live in community and who inform their actions with community spirit by word, action, and example.

Particular circumstances, considered later, may require adjustments, but these should not be such as to remove a

69. John Paul II, to the Plenary Meeting of CICLSAL, November 20, 1992, n. 3, OR (English) December 2, 1992.

70. Cf. *LG* 1.

religious from living the communion and spirit of his or her community.

56. Religious communities, aware of their responsibilities towards the greater fraternity of the Church, also become a sign of the possibility of living Christian fraternity and of the price that must be paid to build any form of fraternal life.

Moreover, in the context of the diverse societies of our planet—torn as they are by the divisive forces of passion and conflicting interests, yearning for unity but unsure of what path to follow—the presence of communities where people of different ages, languages, and cultures meet as brothers and sisters, and which remain united despite the inevitable conflicts and difficulties inherent in common life, is in itself a sign that bears witness to a higher reality and points to higher aspirations.

"Religious communities, who by their life proclaim the joy and the human and supernatural value of Christian fraternity, speak to our society about the transforming power of the Good News."[71]

"And above all these, put on love, which binds everything together in perfect harmony" (*Col* 3:14), love as it was taught and lived by Jesus Christ and communicated to us through his Spirit. This love that unites is also the love that leads us to extend to others the experience of communion with God and with each other. In other words, it creates apostles by urging communities on their path of mission, whether this be contemplative, proclamation of the Word, or ministries of charity. God wishes to inundate the world with his love; so, fraternal communities become missionaries of this love and prophetic signs of its unifying power.

---

71. John Paul II, to the Plenary Meeting of *CICLSAL*, November 20, 1992, n. 4, OR (English) December 2, 1992.

57. The quality of fraternal life has a significant impact on the perseverance of individual religious. Just as the poor quality of fraternal life has been mentioned frequently by many as the reason for leaving religious life, so fraternity lived fully has often been, and still is, a valuable support to the perseverance of many.

Within a truly fraternal community, each member has a sense of co-responsibility for the faithfulness of the others; each one contributes to a serene climate of sharing life, of understanding, and of mutual help; each is attentive to the moments of fatigue, suffering, isolation, or lack of motivation in others; each offers support to those who are saddened by difficulties and trials.

Thus, religious communities, in the support they give to the perseverance of their members, also acquire the value of a sign of the abiding fidelity of God, and thus become a support to the faith and fidelity of Christians who are immersed in the events of this world, where the paths of fidelity seem to be less and less known.

PART III

RELIGIOUS COMMUNITY AS THE PLACE AND SUBJECT OF MISSION

58. Just as the Holy Spirit anointed the Church in the Upper Room to send her out to evangelize the world, so every religious community, as an authentic Pneumatic community of the Risen One, is also, and according to its own nature, apostolic.

In fact, "communion begets communion: essentially it is likened to a mission on behalf of communion.... Communion and mission are profoundly connected with each other, they interpenetrate and mutually imply each other, to the point that communion represents both the source and the fruit of mission: communion gives rise to mission and mission is accomplished in communion."[72]

No religious community, including specifically contemplative ones, is turned in on itself; rather it is announcement, *diakonia*, and prophetic witness. The Risen One, who lives in the community, communicating his own Spirit to it, makes it a witness of the resurrection.

Religious Community and Mission

Before reflecting on some particular situations that religious communities, in order to be faithful to their specific mission, must face today in various contexts around the world, it is helpful to consider here the particular relationship between different kinds of religious communities and the mission they are called to carry out.

---

72. *ChL* 32; cf. *PO* 2.

59. *a)* The Second Vatican Council made the following statement: "Let religious see to it that the Church truly show forth Christ through them with ever-increasing clarity to believers and unbelievers alike—Christ in contemplation on the mountain, or proclaiming the kingdom of God to the multitudes, or healing the sick and maimed and converting sinners to a good life, or blessing children and doing good to all, always in obedience to the will of the Father who sent him."[73]

From participation in the various aspects of Christ's mission, the Spirit makes different religious families arise, characterized by different missions, and therefore by different kinds of community.

b) The contemplative type of community (showing forth Christ on the mountain) is centered on the twofold communion with God and among its members. It has a most efficacious apostolic impact, even though it remains to a great extent hidden in mystery. The "apostolic" religious community (showing forth Christ among the multitudes) is consecrated for active service to others, a service characterized by a specific charism.

Among "apostolic communities," some are more strongly centered on common life so that their apostolate depends on the possibility of their forming community. Others are decidedly oriented towards mission and for them the type of community depends on the type of mission. Institutes clearly ordered to specific forms of apostolic service accent the priority of the entire religious family, considered as one apostolic body and one large community to which the Holy Spirit has given a mission to be carried out in the Church. The communion which vivifies and gathers the large family is lived concretely in the single local

---

73. *LG* 46a.

communities, which are entrusted with carrying out the mission, according to the different needs.

There are thus various kinds of religious community that have been handed down over the centuries, such as monastic, conventual, and active or "diaconal."

It follows that "common life lived in community" does not have the same meaning for all religious. Monastics, conventuals and religious of active life have maintained legitimate differences in their ways of understanding and living religious community.

This diversity is presented in their constitutions, which outline the character of the institute, and thus the character of the religious community.

c) It is generally recognized, especially for religious communities dedicated to works of the apostolate, that it proves to be somewhat difficult in daily experience to balance community and apostolic commitment. If it is dangerous to oppose these two aspects, it is also difficult to harmonize them. This too is a fruitful tension of religious life, which is designed to cultivate simultaneously both the *disciple* who must live with Jesus and with the group of those following him and the *apostle* who must take part in the mission of the Lord.

d) In recent years, the great variety of apostolic needs has often resulted in coexistence, within one institute, of communities considerably different from each other: large and rather structured communities exist alongside smaller, much more flexible ones, but without losing the authentic community character of religious life.

All of this has a considerable impact on the life of the institute and on its makeup, which is now no longer as compact as it once was, but is more diversified and has different ways of living religious community.

e) The tendency, in some institutes, to emphasize mission over community, and to favor diversity over unity, has had a profound impact on fraternal life in common, to the point that this has become, at times, almost an option rather than an integral part of religious life.

The consequences of this have certainly not been positive; they lead us to ask serious questions about the appropriateness of continuing along this path, and suggest the need to undertake a path of rediscovering the intimate bond between community and mission, in order creatively to overcome unilateral tendencies, which invariably impoverish the rich reality of religious life.

In the Particular Church

60. The missionary presence of a religious community is developed within the context of a particular Church, to which the members bring the richness of their consecration, of their fraternal life, and of their charism.

By its mere presence, not only does a religious community bear in itself the richness of Christian life but as a unit it constitutes a particularly effective announcement of the Christian message. It can be said that it is a living and continuous preaching. This objective condition, which clearly holds religious themselves responsible, calling them to be faithful to this, their primary mission, correcting and eliminating anything which could attenuate or weaken the drawing power of their example, makes their presence in the particular Church identifiable and precious, prior to any other consideration.

Since charity is the greatest of the charisms (cf. *1 Cor* 13:13), a religious community enriches the Church of which it is a living part, first of all by its love. It loves the universal Church and the particular Church in which it is inserted because it is within the Church and as Church that it is placed in contact with the communion of the blessed and beatifying Trinity, source of all goods. In this way it becomes a privileged manifestation of the very nature of the Church herself.

A religious community loves the particular Church, enriches it with its charisms and opens it to a more universal dimension. The delicate relationships between the pastoral needs of the particular Church and the charismatic specificity of the religious community have been dealt with in *Mutuae Relationes*. In addition to the theological and pastoral orientations it provides, that document has made an important contribution to more cordial and intense collaboration. The time has come to take another look at that document, in order to give a new thrust to the spirit of true communion between religious community and the particular Church.

The growing difficulties of mission work and the scarcity of personnel can tempt both a religious community and the particular Church to a certain isolation; this, of course, does nothing to improve mutual understanding and collaboration.

The religious community runs the risk, on the one hand, of being present in the particular Church with no organic link to its life or to its pastoral program and, on the other hand, of being reduced to merely pastoral functions. Moreover, if religious life tends more and more to emphasize its own charismatic identity, the local Church often makes pressing and insistent demands on the energies of religious for the pastoral activities of the diocese or parish. The guidelines provided by *Mutuae Relationes* take us far from the isolation and independence of a religious community in relation to a particular Church and far from the practical assimilation of a religious community into the particular Church.

Just as a religious community cannot act independently of the particular Church, or as an alternative to it, or much less against the directives and pastoral program of the particular Church, so the particular Church cannot dispose, according to its own pleasure and according to its needs, of a religious community or of any of its members.

It is important to recall that a lack of proper consideration for the charism of a religious community serves neither the good of the particular Church nor that of the religious community itself. Only if a religious community has a well-defined charismatic identity can it integrate itself into an "overall pastoral program" without losing its own character. Indeed, only in this way will it enrich the program with its gift.

We must not forget that every charism is born in the Church and for the world and the link to its source and purpose must be continuously renewed; each charism is alive to the extent that one is faithful to it.

The Church and the world make possible its interpretation, request it and stimulate it to continued growth in relevance and vitality. Charism and particular Church should not be in conflict but should rather support and complete one another, especially now that so many problems of living out the charism and its insertion into changed situations have arisen.

At the root of many misunderstandings is perhaps a mutual partial knowledge either of the particular Church or of religious life, and of the responsibilities of the bishop for religious life.

It is earnestly recommended that all diocesan theological seminaries include a course specifically on the theology of consecrated life, including study of its dogmatic, juridic and pastoral aspects; religious should in turn receive adequate theological formation concerning the particular Church.[74]

---

74. Cf. *MR* 30b, 47.

Above all, however, a truly fraternal religious community will feel in duty bound to spread a climate of communion that will enable the entire Christian community to consider itself "the family of the children of God."

61. *The Parish*

In parishes, it may sometimes be difficult to coordinate parish life and community life.

In some regions, the difficulties of living in community while being active in parish ministry create considerable tension for religious priests. At times, the heavy commitment to pastoral work in the parish is carried out to the detriment of the institute's charism and to community life, to the point that parishioners, secular clergy, and even religious themselves lose sight of the particular nature of religious life.

Urgent pastoral needs must never lead us to forget that the best service a religious community can give to the Church is that of being faithful to its charism. This is also reflected in accepting responsibility for parishes and running them. Preference should be given to parishes which allow a community to live as community and where the religious can express their charism.

Religious communities of women, also frequently asked to become involved in a more direct way in the pastoral ministry of the parish, go through similar difficulties.

Here too, it is worth repeating, their presence will be all the more fruitful, the more the religious community is present in its charismatic character.[75] All of this can be a great advantage for both the religious community and the pastoral work, in which religious women are generally well accepted and appreciated.

---

75. *MR* 49-50.

62. *Ecclesial Movements*

Ecclesial movements in the broadest sense of the term, endowed with lively spirituality and apostolic vitality, have attracted the attention of some religious who have become involved in them, sometimes deriving fruits of spiritual renewal, apostolic dedication and a reawakening of their vocation. Sometimes, however, such involvements have also brought divisions into the religious community.

It is, then, opportune to make the following observations:

a) some movements are simply movements of renewal; others have apostolic projects which can be incompatible with those of a religious community.

Also, there can be different degrees of involvement on the part of consecrated persons: some take part only as onlookers; others participate occasionally; still others are permanent members while remaining in full harmony with their own community and spirituality. However, those whose principal membership goes to the movement and who become psychologically distanced from their own institute become a problem. They live in a state of inner division: they dwell within their communities, but they live in accordance with the pastoral plans and guidelines of the movement.

There is need, then, for careful discernment between one movement and another, and between various kinds of involvement on the part of individual religious;

b) these movements can be a fruitful challenge to a religious community, to its spiritual dynamic, to the quality of its prayer life, to the relevance of its apostolic initiatives, to its fidelity to the Church, to the intensity of its fraternal life. A religious community should be open to encounters with these movements, showing an attitude of mutual recognition, dialogue and exchange of gifts.

The great spiritual tradition—ascetic and mystical—of religious life and of the institute can also be helpful to these young movements;

c) the main difficulty in relating to these movements is the identity of the individual consecrated person: if it is solid, the relationship can be fruitful for both.

For those religious who seem to live more in and for a particular movement than in and for their religious community, it is good to recall the following statement in *Potissimum Insitutionis:* "An institute...has an internal cohesiveness which it receives from its nature, its end, its spirit, its character, and its traditions. This whole patrimony is the axis around which both the identity and unity of the institute itself and the unity of life of each of its members are maintained. This is a gift of the Spirit to the Church and does not admit any interference or any admixture. A dialogue and sharing within the Church presumes that each institute is well aware of what it is.

"Candidates for the religious life...place themselves...under the authority of the superiors [of the institute].... They cannot simultaneously be dependent upon someone apart from the institute....

"These exigencies remain after the religious profession, so as to avoid appearance of divided loyalties, either on the level of the personal spiritual life of the religious or on the level of their mission."[76]

Taking part in a movement will be positive for religious if it reinforces their specific identity.

---

76. *PI* 93.

Some Particular Situations

63. *Insertion into Poor Neighborhoods*

Alongside many other brothers and sisters in the faith, religious communities have been among the first in attending to the material and spiritual poverty of their time, in continuously renewed ways.

In recent years, poverty has been an issue which has involved religious very intensely and which has touched their hearts. Religious life has seriously faced the question of how to be available for the task of evangelizing the poor *(evangelizare pauperibus)*. But religious have also wanted to be evangelized through their contact with the world of the poor *(evangelizari a pauperibus)*.

In this huge mobilization, in which religious have chosen as their program "everyone for the poor," "many with the poor," "some like the poor," some accomplishments in the area of being "like the poor" deserve special mention.

In face of the impoverishment of great masses of people, especially in abandoned and marginal areas of large cities and in forgotten rural areas, "religious communities of insertion" have arisen as one of the expressions of the preferential and solitary evangelical option for the poor. These communities intend to accompany the poor in their process of integral liberation, but are also fruit of the desire to discover the poor Christ in marginalized brothers and sisters, in order to serve him and become conformed to him.

a) "Insertion" as an ideal of religious life has developed in a context of the movement of faith and solidarity of religious communities with the poorest.

It is a reality which cannot but arouse admiration for the tremendous personal dedication and great sacrifices which it involves; for the love of the poor which carries one to share their real and harsh poverty; for the effort to make the Gospel present in sectors of the population which are without hope; to bring them closer to the Word of God, and to make them feel a living part of the Church.[77] These communities often live in areas deeply marked by a violence which gives rise to insecurity and, sometimes, to persecution, to the point of real danger to life. Their great courage is clear testimony to the hope that it is possible to live as brothers and sisters, despite all situations of suffering and injustice.

Often sent to the front lines of mission, sometimes witnesses of the apostolic creativity of their founders, such religious communities ought to be able to count on the good will and fraternal prayer of the other members of their institute and on particular care from their superiors.[78]

b) These religious communities should not be left to themselves; they must be helped to live a life of community. This requires space for prayer and fraternal exchanges, in order to ensure that the charismatic originality of their institute not appear to them relatively less important than undifferentiated service to the poor, and in order that their evangelical witness not he clouded by partisan interpretations or exploitations.[79]

Superiors shall be careful to select suitable members and to prepare such communities in a way that will ensure connection with other communities of the institute, thereby guaranteeing continuity.

---

77. Cf. *SD* 85.
78. Cf. *RHP* 6; *EN* 69; *SD* 92.
79. Cf. *PI* 28.

c) We should also applaud the efforts of the other religious communities who are effectively committed to the poor, whether in traditional ways, or in new ways more suited to new forms of poverty, or by raising awareness at all levels of society of the problems of the poor—thus generating among the laity vocations to social and political commitment, charitable projects and voluntary service.

All of this bears witness that the faith is alive in the Church, that the love of Christ is active and present among the poor: "as you did it to one of the least of these, you did it to me" (cf. *Mt* 25:40).

Where insertion among the poor has become, for both the poor and the religious community itself, a true experience of God, there is experienced the truth of the affirmation that the poor are evangelized and the poor evangelize.

64. *Small Communities*

a) Other social factors have also influenced communities. In some more economically developed regions, the state has become more active in areas such as education, health and social services, often in ways that leave little or no space for other agents, such as religious communities. On the other hand, the decrease in numbers of men and women religious and, here or there, a limited understanding of the presence of Catholics in social action, seen more as supplementary rather than as a genuine expression of Christian charity, have made it difficult to carry on complex projects.

Hence, in some regions, there has been a gradual abandonment of traditional works—which for many years had been in the hands of strong and homogeneous communities—and an increase in small communities available for new kinds of services, more often than not in keeping with the institute's charism.

b) Smaller communities have also become more frequent as a result of deliberate choices made by certain institutes in order to promote fraternal union and collaboration through closer relationships among persons and a mutual and more broadly based sharing of responsibility.

Such communities, as mentioned in *Evangelica Testificatio*,[80] are certainly possible, although they have proved to be more demanding for their members.

c) Small communities, often situated in close contact with the daily life and problems of people—but also more exposed to the influence of a secularized mentality—have the important responsibility of being visible places of happy fraternity, enthusiastic industry and transcendent hope.

It is therefore necessary that these communities be given a program of life which is solid, flexible and binding, approved by the competent authority who is to ensure that the apostolate have a community dimension. This program should be suited to the persons and demands of the mission in such a way as to promote balance between prayer and activity, between moments of community intimacy and apostolic work. It should also include regular meetings with other communities of the same institute, precisely to overcome the danger of isolation and margination from the broader community of the institute.

d) Even if small communities can offer advantages, it is not normally recommended that an institute be made up of only small communities. Larger communities are necessary. They can offer significant services both to the entire institute and to the smaller communities: cultivating the life of prayer and

---

80. Cf. *ET* 40.

celebrations with more intensity and richness, being preferred places for study and reflection, offering possibilities for retreat and rest for members working on the more difficult frontiers of the evangelizing mission.

This exchange between the two kinds of community is made fruitful by a climate of kindness and acceptance.

These communities should be recognizable primarily for the fraternal love which unites the members, for the simplicity of their lives, for the mission they undertake in the name of the community, for persevering fidelity to their charism, for the constant diffusion of the "sweet perfume" of Christ (*2 Cor* 2:15), so that in the most diverse circumstances they may point to the "way of peace," even for the confused and fragmented members of modern society.

65. *Men and Women Religious Living Alone*

One of the realities encountered from time to time is that of men and women religious living alone. Common life in a house of the institute is essential for religious life. "Religious should live in their own religious house, observing a common life. They should not live alone without serious reason, and should not do so if there is a community of their institute reasonably near."[81]

There are, however, exceptions which must be evaluated and can be authorized by superiors[82] by reason of apostolate on behalf of the institute (as for example, commitments requested by the Church; extraordinary missions; great distances in mission territories; gradual decrease in the membership of a community, to the point that a single religious is in charge of one of the institute's works), or for reasons of health and study.

---

81. *EE* III, § 12.
82. Cf. can. 665 § 1.

While it is the responsibility of superiors to cultivate frequent contacts with members living outside community, it is the duty of these religious to keep alive in themselves the sense of belonging to the institute and a sense of communion with its members, seeking every means suitable for strengthening fraternal bonds. Periods of intense communal living must be scheduled, as well as regular meetings with fellow religious for formation, fraternal sharing, review of life, and prayer, for breathing in a family atmosphere. Wherever they may be, members of an institute should be bearers of the charism of their religious family.

A religious living alone is never an ideal. The norm is that religious live in fraternal communities: the individual is consecrated in this common life and it is in this form of life that such men and women normally undertake their apostolate; it is to this life that they return, in heart and in person, as often as it is necessary for them to live apart for a time, long or short.

a) The demands of a particular apostolic work, for example of a diocesan work, have led various institutes to send one of their members to collaborate in an inter-congregational team. There are positive experiences in which religious who collaborate in serving a particular work in a place where there is no community of their own institute, instead of living alone, live in the same house, pray together, have meetings to reflect on the word of God, share food and domestic duties, etc. As long as this does not become a substitute for living communication with their own institute, this kind of "community life" can be advantageous for the work and for the religious themselves.

Religious should be prudent in wanting to take on work which normally requires them to live outside community, and superiors should likewise be prudent in assigning members to these works.

b) Also, requests for attending to elderly and sick parents, often involving long absences from community, need careful discernment and possibly such needs can be satisfied by other arrangements in order to avoid excessively long absences of the son or daughter.

c) It must be noted that the religious who lives alone, without an assignment or permission from the superior, is fleeing from the obligation to common life. Nor is it sufficient to take part in a few meetings or celebrations to be fully a religious. Efforts must be made to bring about the progressive disappearance of these unjustified and inadmissible situations for religious men and women.

d) In each case, it is helpful to recall that religious, even when living outside community, are subject in areas relating to apostolate to the authority of the bishop,[83] who is to be informed of their presence in his diocese.

e) Should there be institutes in which, unfortunately, the majority of members no longer live in community, such institutes would no longer be able to be considered true religious institutes. Superiors and religious are invited to reflect seriously on this sorrowful outcome and, consequently, on the importance of resuming with vigor the practice of fraternal life in common.

66. *In Mission Territories*

Fraternal life in common has special value in areas of the mission *ad gentes* because it shows the world, especially the non-Christian world, the "newness" of Christianity, that is, the charity which is capable of overcoming divisions created by race, color, tribe. In some countries where the Gospel cannot be

---

83. Cf. can. 678 § 1.

proclaimed, religious communities are almost the only sign and silent and effective witness of Christ and of the Church.

But not rarely it is precisely in mission territories that religious come up against notable practical difficulties in building stable and viable communities: distances which require great mobility and widely scattered communities; belonging to different races, tribes, and cultures; the need for formation in inter-congregational centers. These and other factors can be obstacles for a community ideal.

The important thing is that the members of the institute be aware of the unusualness of the situation, that they promote frequent communication among themselves, that they promote regular community meetings and, as soon as possible, set up fraternal religious communities with a strong missionary character so that they can offer the missionary sign *par excellence:* "that they may all be one..., so that the world may believe" (*Jn* 17:21).

67. *Reorganization of Works*

Changes in cultural and ecclesial conditions, internal factors in the development of institutes and changes of their resources can require a reorganization of the works and of the presence of religious communities.

This task, not an easy one, has real implications touching on community. Generally, it is a question of works in which many brothers and sisters have expended their best apostolic energies and to which they are tied by special psychological and spiritual bonds.

The future of these works, their apostolic significance and their reorganization require study, comparison and discernment. All of this can become a school for learning to seek and follow the will of God, but at the same time it can be an occasion of painful conflicts not easily overcome.

Criteria which cannot be overlooked and which enlighten communities at the time of decisions, sometimes bold and painful, are: commitment to safeguard the significance of their own charism in a specific setting, concern to keep alive an authentic fraternal life and attention to the needs of the particular Church. A trusting and ongoing dialogue with the particular Church is therefore essential, as is effective connection with those responsible for communion among the religious.

In addition to attention to the needs of the particular Church, religious communities must be concerned also for all that the world neglects—that is to say, for the new forms of poverty and suffering in the many forms in which they are found in different parts of the world.

Reorganization will be creative and a source of prophetic signs if it takes care to announce new ways of being present— even if only in small numbers—in order to respond to new needs, especially those of the most abandoned and forgotten areas.

68. *Elderly Religious*

One of the situations which community life faces more often today is the increasing age of its members. Aging has taken on particular significance both because of the reduced number of new vocations and because of the progress of medicine.

For a community, on the one hand, this fact means concern for accepting in their midst and esteeming deeply the presence and services which elderly brothers and sisters can offer and, on the other, it means attention to provide fraternally and in a way consistent with consecrated life those means of spiritual and material assistance which the elderly need.

The presence of the elderly in communities can be quite positive. An elderly religious who does not allow himself or herself to be overcome by the annoyances and limitations of age, but keeps alive joy, love and hope, is an invaluable support for the young. The elderly provide a witness, wisdom, and prayer which are a constant encouragement to the young in their spiritual and apostolic journey. Moreover, religious who take care of the elderly give evangelical credibility to their own institute as a "true family convoked in the name of the Lord."[84]

Consecrated persons also should prepare themselves long in advance for becoming old and for extending their "active" years, by learning to discover their new way of building community and collaborating in the common mission, responding positively to the challenges of their age, through lively spiritual and cultural interests, by prayer, and by continued participation in their work for as long as they can render service, even if limited. Superiors should arrange courses and meetings to assist personal preparation and to prolong and enhance as much as possible the presence of religious in their normal workplaces.

When in time these elderly members lose their autonomy or require special care, even when their health is cared for by lay persons, the institute should be very much concerned with supporting them so that they continue to feel a part of the life of the institute, sharers in its mission, involved in its apostolic dynamism, comforted in their solitude, encouraged in their suffering. They never leave the mission but they are placed at its heart, participating in it in a new and effective manner.

However invisible, their fruitfulness is not less than that of more active communities. These derive strength and fruitfulness from the prayer, the suffering, and the apparent lack of influence

---

84. *PC* 15a.

of the elderly. Mission has need of both, and the fruits will become visible when the Lord comes in glory with his angels.

69. Problems posed by the growing number of elderly religious become still more striking in some monasteries which have suffered a lack of vocations. Because a monastery is normally an autonomous community, it is difficult for it to overcome these problems by itself. So it is helpful to recall the importance of organisms of communion, such as federations, for example, in order to overcome situations of great need of personnel.

Fidelity to the contemplative life requires the members of a monastery to unite with another monastery of the same Order when a monastic community, by reason of the number of its members, age, or lack of vocations, foresees its own extinction. Also in the painful situation of communities no longer able to live according to their proper vocation because the members are worn down by practical labors or by caring for the elderly or sick members, it will be necessary to seek reinforcements from the same Order or to choose union or fusion with another monastery.[85]

70. *New Relationship to the Laity*

Conciliar ecclesiology has shed light on the complementarity of the different vocations in the Church which are called to be, together in every situation and place, witnesses of the Risen Lord. Encounter and collaboration among religious men, religious women, and lay faithful are seen as an example of ecclesial communion and, at the same time, they strengthen apostolic energies for the evangelization of the world.

---

85. Cf. *PC* 21 and 22.

Appropriate contact between the values characteristic of the lay vocation, such as a more concrete perception of the life of the world, of culture, politics, economy, etc., and the values characteristic of religious life, such as the radicality of the following of Christ, the contemplative and eschatological dimension of Christian existence, etc., can become a fruitful exchange of gifts between the lay faithful and religious communities.

Collaboration and exchange of gifts become more intense when groups of lay persons share, by vocation and in the way proper to them, in the heart of the same spiritual family, in the charism and mission of the institute. In this way, fruitful relationships, based on bonds of mature co-responsibility and supported by regularly scheduled programs of formation in the spirituality of the institute will be established.

In order to achieve such an objective, however, it is necessary to have: religious communities with a clear charismatic identity, assimilated and lived, capable of transmitting them to others and disposed to share them; religious communities with an intense spirituality and missionary enthusiasm for communicating the same spirit and the same evangelizing thrust; religious communities who know how to animate and encourage lay people to share the charism of their institute, according to their secular character and according to their different style of life, inviting them to discover new ways of making the same charism and mission operative. In this way, a religious community becomes a center radiating outwardly, a spiritual force, a center of animation, of fraternity creating fraternity, and of communion and ecclesial collaboration, where the different contributions of each help build up the Body of Christ, which is the Church.

Naturally, very close collaboration should be worked out with respect for the reciprocal vocations and different styles of life proper to religious and to lay persons.

A religious community has its own needs of animation, horarium, discipline and privacy,[86] such as to render unacceptable those forms of collaboration which imply cohabitation and the living together of religious and laity, even when such arrangements specify conditions which are to be respected.

Otherwise, a religious community would lose its own character, which it is responsible for maintaining by observing its common life.

---

86. Cf. can. 667, 607 § 3.

CONCLUSION

71. A religious community, as an expression of the Church, is a fruit of the Spirit and a participation in the Trinitarian communion. For this reason, each and every religious is committed to feel co-responsible for fraternal life in common, so that it will manifest clearly their belonging to Christ, who chooses and calls brothers and sisters to live together in his name.

"The effectiveness of religious life depends on the quality of the fraternal life in common. Even more so, the current renewal in the Church and in religious life is characterized by a search for communion and community."[87]

For some consecrated persons and for some communities, the task of beginning again to rebuild fraternal life in common may appear daunting, even utopian. In the face of certain past wounds and of difficulties in the present, the task may appear beyond feeble human capacities.

It is a question of taking up in faith a reflection on the theological sense of fraternal life in common, of being convinced that through it the witness of consecration flows.

"The response to this invitation to build community together with the Lord, in patience every day," says our Holy Father,

---

87. John Paul II, to the Plenary Meeting of *CICLSAL*, November 20, 1992, n. 3, *OR* (English) December 2, 1992.

"takes place on the way of the Cross; it requires frequent self-denial."[88]

United with Mary, Mother of Jesus, our communities invoke the Spirit, who has the power to create fraternal communities which radiate the joy of the Gospel and which are capable of attracting new disciples, following the example of the earliest community: "and they devoted themselves to the apostles' teaching and fellowship, to the breaking of bread and the prayers" (*Acts* 2:42), "and more than ever believers were added to the Lord, multitudes both of men and women" (*Acts* 5:14).

May Mary bring together religious communities and support them daily in invoking the Spirit, who is the bond, the ferment, and the source of all fraternal communion.

On January 15, 1994, the Holy Father approved this document of the Congregation for Institutes of Consecrated Life and Societies of Apostolic Life and authorized its publication.

Rome, February 2, 1994,
Feast of the Presentation of the Lord.

Eduardo Cardinal Martinez Somalo
Prefect

+ Francisco Javier Errázuriz Ossa
Secretary

---

88. *Ibid.*, n. 2.

ALASKA
750 West 5th Ave., Anchorage, AK 99501; 907-272-8183

CALIFORNIA
3908 Sepulveda Blvd., Culver City, CA 90230; 310-397-8676
5945 Balboa Ave., San Diego, CA 92111; 619-565-9181
46 Geary Street, San Francisco, CA 94108; 415-781-5180

FLORIDA
145 S.W. 107th Ave., Miami, FL 33174; 305-559-6715

HAWAII
1143 Bishop Street, Honolulu, HI 96813; 808-521-2731

ILLINOIS
172 North Michigan Ave., Chicago, IL 60601; 312-346-4228

LOUISIANA
4403 Veterans Memorial Blvd., Metairie, LA 70006; 504-887-7631

MASSACHUSETTS
50 St. Paul's Ave., Jamaica Plain, Boston, MA 02130; 617-522-8911
Rte. 1, 885 Providence Hwy., Dedham, MA 02026; 617-326-5385

MISSOURI
9804 Watson Rd., St. Louis, MO 63126; 314-965-3512

NEW JERSEY
561 U.S. Route 1, Wick Plaza, Edison, NJ 08817; 908-572-1200

NEW YORK
150 East 52nd Street, New York, NY 10022; 212-754-1110
78 Fort Place, Staten Island, NY 10301; 718-447-5071

OHIO
2105 Ontario Street, Cleveland, OH 44115; 216-621-9427

PENNSYLVANIA
Northeast Shopping Center, 9171-A Roosevelt Blvd. (between Grant Ave.
& Welsh Rd.), Philadelphia, PA 19114; 610-277-7728

SOUTH CAROLINA
243 King Street, Charleston, SC 29401; 803-577-0175

TENNESSEE
4811 Poplar Ave., Memphis, TN 38117; 901-761-2987

TEXAS
114 Main Plaza, San Antonio, TX 78205; 210-224-8101

VIRGINIA
1025 King Street, Alexandria, VA 22314; 703-549-3806

GUAM
285 Farenholt Ave., Suite 308, Tamuning, Guam 96911; 671-649-4377

CANADA
3022 Dufferin Street, Toronto, Ontario, Canada M6B 3T5; 416-781-9131